"The Art of Storytelling
By: Richard Douglas Krause

The Art of Storytelling

Richard Krause

Published by Richard Krause, 2024.

The Art of Storytelling
Copyright © 2024 by Richard Douglas Krause
All rights reserved, including the right to reproduce this book or portions thereof in any form.

While every precaution has been taken in the preparation of this book, the publisher assumes no responsibility for errors or omissions, or for damages resulting from the use of the information contained herein.

THE ART OF STORYTELLING

First edition. November 10, 2024.

Copyright © 2024 Richard Krause.

ISBN: 979-8227613479

Written by Richard Krause.

Table of Contents

Introduction 1
Chapter 1 The Power of Stories 7
Chapter 2: The Anatomy of a Story 17
Chapter 3: Creating Compelling Characters 31
Chapter 4: Mastering Plot and Structure 43
Chapter 5: The Art of Setting 57
Chapter 6: Dialogue that Sings 67
Chapter 7: Harnessing Conflict and Tension 79
Chapter 8: Exploring Themes and Meaning 93
Chapter 9: The Art of Storytelling Across Mediums 105
Chapter 10: The Writer's Journey 115

Introduction

What's the oldest tradition shared by every single culture across the entire globe throughout human history? Yep, you guessed it - storytelling.

Before we even developed written languages or advanced technologies, we humans have been crafting engaging narratives to entertain each other, preserve our histories and cultural identities, and grapple with the profoundly bewildering experience of simply being alive as conscious creatures. Storytelling arguably shaped the very foundations of human civilization and cognition itself.

Think about it, how did those ancient proto-humans first start developing more abstract thought, language abilities, and a sense of self and community beyond mere base survival instincts? By sharing stories around the crackling campfire as night fell, of course! Transforming the raw sensory data of their daily experiences out in that harsh, unforgiving prehistoric world into narratives laced with meaning that helped spark the evolutionary leap that set our species on the path to self-awareness and all of civilization's mind-boggling achievements.

Every epic myth you've ever heard, whether ancient Greek classics like The Odyssey, traditional Indigenous tales like the Navajo's DinéBahane', Arabian Nights fables, or Hindu Vedic narratives, they all originated from those prehistoric storytelling circles. Our ancestors wove imaginative yarns to explain the natural world's baffling phenomena, inspire moral behaviors that allowed organized societies to flourish, preserve their rich cultural legacies across generations, and essentially birth humanity's very consciousness and cognitive capabilities.

From that profound primordial tradition bloomed all the incredible narrative arts and entertainment that have enriched cultures the world over for thousands of years. Every form of storytelling we enjoy today, compelling novels, captivating TV dramas, stunning motion pictures, imaginative comic books, immersive video games, they all tap into those very same hardwired neural circuits for mythmaking that lurk within our ancient human brains.

You see, storytelling isn't just some quaint primitive tradition, it's fundamentally woven into the very fabric of our species' evolution and psychology. Our reality, modeling minds crave narratives to make sense of all the beautiful, harsh, ambiguous, and profound elements of existing as a thinking, feeling, and conscious entity. That's why we tell stories in every conceivable artform and creative medium available! It's our uniquely human way of grappling with the Big Questions.

Stories provide the indispensable conceptual metaphors and mythologies that help us explore the imponderables fueling existential dread and spiritual wonder since the dawn of human self-awareness: Where did everything come from? What happens when we shuffle off this mortal coil? Why are we here at all experiencing the bizarre phenomena of subjective conscious existence within a cold, monolithic universe of matter and energy that simply exists with no deeper purpose or story of its own?

Ancient myths gifted our human minds a framework of meaning to contextualize and process these daunting existential quandaries through compelling narratives of gods, heroes, allegories and imagined realms beyond the physical world. Today's cutting-edge sci-fi tales use speculative fiction to explore potential technological immortalities and cosmic truths. At our core, all these spiritual wonderings and philosophical enigmas arise from the same deeply ingrained human compulsion: the quest to craft unifying stories that lend purpose and profundity to our bizarre existence.

Of course, storytelling isn't solely about pondering the heavy stuff; it's also one of our most powerful tools for entertainment, emotional engagement, and channeling the heights of creativity and expression. From dazzling literary fiction that unveils the incredible kaleidoscope of human experiences and insights into ourselves, to escapist adventure stories that transport us to epic worlds of unbridled imagination, to intimate personal narratives mining soulful interiority and emotional resonance, stories manifest the staggering range of what our remarkable human minds can conceive and communicate to one another.

Stories build empathy by placing us within other subjective experiences, cultures and identities we'd never otherwise intimately understand. They reframe complex history and events through compelling narrative lenses that render abstract data into vivid illuminations of the humanity behind the facts. They articulate heartfelt universal truths about love, loss, identity, purpose, death and every other facet of existence in a way that cuts to the core emotional resonance that dry analyses so often miss.

That's the true magic of stories, their power to encapsulate entire lived realities spanning generations within meticulously crafted emotional arcs and symbolic narrative meaning resonating straight into our very essences. Whether you're immersed in an eye-opening literary fiction novel, a sweeping Emmy-winning TV saga, an inspirational biopic, or a groundbreaking interactive video game narrative, you're receiving a profound cognitive download of concentrated truth and artistry capable of shifting your very perception of self and reality itself in ways nothing else can match.

Stories don't simply entertain, they're a synapse sparking injection of distilled human wisdom and philosophy made tangible through the elemental art forms of character, conflict, setting, plot and theme. When fashioned by a skilled storyteller's deft hand, even the most audacious tales tapping speculative genres like sci-fi or fantasy become clarifying mirrors reflecting back revelations about the authentic human condition buried within their imaginative metaphors and parable like structures.

Essentially, storytelling represents one of our species' most distinctively powerful cognitive superpowers as conscious beings. While other lifeforms may achieve rudimentary reasoning or awareness, we're the only ones who've mastered the singular creative ability of crafting symbolic narratives and contextual frameworks to find deeper meaning, truth and expression within the maelstrom of subjective experience constantly inundating our waking minds.

Our brains churn out anecdotes and storified interpretations as comprehensible "best fit" models of existence itself. That's why no single belief system, philosophy or worldview can ever hope to encapsulate the totality of all felt human truths throughout history and across cultures, only the boundless, ever-expanding multiverse of story possesses sufficient flexibility and diversity to reflect the full prism of subjective experiences making up our vast shared consciousness.

So whether you're an aspiring novelist burning to immerse readers within new literary realms, an auteur filmmaker crafting mind-bending cinematic experiences to both entertain and enlighten, a veteran stage actor masterfully breathing life into characters that grip audiences with their raw human truth, or simply a voracious consumer of every captivating narrative art form imaginable, make no mistake that you're engaging with one of the most vital, essentially human activities connecting all of us Earthly voyagers drifting together through deep space on our pale blue lifeboat.

Storytelling isn't just an entertaining diversion or intellectual exercise;it forges the neural superhighways linking our inner realms of imagination and experience into a vibrant consensus reality of symbolic exchange between human minds. Stories birth shared context from individual isolation, manifesting the very essence of culture, art, and the wondrous strange journey of our cosmic journey as a self-aware species.

And within these pages, I'll be your guide exploring the indispensable craft behind shaping compelling tales capable of burrowing into the core of a reader's consciousness. I'll be sharing insights into mastering the archetypal elements like character, plot, dialogue, narrative structure, theme and more that have formed the molecular foundations for transcendent stories spanning all eras and cultures.

You'll gain a deeper appreciation for the profound purpose and cognitive "magic" stories spark within us by deconstructing their functioning on a symbolic, psychological and philosophical level. We'll dive into how masterfully crafted narrative experiences achieve a kind of emotional alchemy by transmuting the messy ambiguities of the human experience into resonant meaning and truth through the metaphorical lens of artful storytelling.

Most importantly, you'll develop your own storytelling muscles by practicing concrete techniques to evoke awe, wonder, visceral thrills, belly laughs, empathetic connections and those singular narrative epiphanies that linger with you the rest of your journey. So study up on these hallowed arts of the storytelling tradition, your consciousness and creativity are about to level up like never before as you join the venerable lineage of spinners of spells, tellers of tales, and Dreamweaver's extraordinaire.

Chapter 1 The Power of Stories

The importance of storytelling throughout human history
Stories have been a huge part of human culture basically since the dawn of time. Think about it, before we had the written word, how do you think important knowledge and histories got passed down? Through storytelling of course!

From cave drawings depicting hunts, to ancient mythological tales attempting to explain things like the sun, moon, seasons and natural phenomena, all the way up through today's books, movies, TV shows, podcasts, and video games, storytelling has been how we humans share information and experiences in an engaging way.

The earliest stories were likely just oral traditions, tales told over campfires and at gatherings, reworked and retold by each new storyteller who breathed fresh life into them. These stories helped preserve cultural beliefs, laws, life lessons and more from generation to generation before there was any way to write this important stuff down permanently.

As language and writing systems developed, some of the first major written works ended up being epic poems and myths from various ancient civilizations around the world. Stories like The Epic of Gilgamesh from Mesopotamia, the Hindu sacred texts like the Vedas, the Greek classics by Homer and other ancient writers. These captured and preserved the beliefs, adventures and cultural identities of entire peoples.

Throughout history, storytelling has helped bind communities and cultures together with a sense of shared narratives and values. Fables and parables used stories as teaching tools to convey moral lessons. Historical accounts and stories about significant heroes and events shaped nations' and peoples' understandings of their roots and respective places in the world.

Even as we became a modern, scientific society, storytelling remained crucial. Some of the most significant developments in human knowledge have been conveyed or explained through story format. From Galileo's clever storytelling techniques to help the public understand his revolutionary theories about the solar system and laws of physics, to scientists like Richard Feynman crafting engaging stories to communicate complex topics like quantum mechanics.

Today, stories continue to be massively important to human society and culture. As technology and media evolves, new mediums and platforms for storytelling have emerged, from centuries old novels and stage plays to recent inventions like movies, TV, video games, podcasts and more. But the core appeal remains the same. We're wired to learn from and be entertained by well-crafted narratives.

Through stories, we understand each other's beliefs, experiences and perspectives across cultures and identities. Great stories build empathy and allow us to see the world through someone else's eyes in a powerful, impactful way that sticks with you. At the same time, stories provide thought provoking commentary and insights into the human condition, society, and our place in the world.

Stories teach us universal truths and life lessons in memorable, compelling ways that dry facts and figures just can't match. They transport us through soaring imagination and creativity to explore new ideas. Their emotional resonance and ability to unite us under shared experiences and understandings make stories vital connective tissue that brings people together across seemingly insurmountable divides.

Without stories, our cultures and histories could easily be forgotten. Records and dry facts alone can't capture the depth of human experiences and truths that have shaped us. Stories give vivid color and profound meaning to the world around us and our existence within it.

Storytelling is truly one of the most fundamentally human capabilities we have. From our ancient ancestors huddled around campfires to modern day couch potatoes binge watching the latest TV obsession, it's the oral tradition of storytelling that defines our shared hopes, fears, triumphs and struggles across geography and time as a species. Stories are how we process, communicate and make sense of the world and our place within it as conscious, thinking beings. Without them, we'd be a sadly diminished culture indeed.

How stories shape our understanding of the world

Stories don't just entertain us, they literally shape how we perceive and make sense of reality itself. The narratives we absorb powerfully influence our thoughts, beliefs and worldviews in profound ways, whether we realize it or not.

Think about it, before you ever learned history from textbooks, you likely first understood major historical events through the lens of stories. The American Revolution was framed as brave underdogs fighting for freedom against oppressive tyrants. Ancient Greece and Rome were brought to life through epic myths and tales of heroes and gods rather than dry facts and figures.

These narratives gave the cold hard data of history a meaningful framework and context that helped it all click into place in our minds. We remember the general storylines and thematic lessons long after the specifics fade. The core understandings and perspectives those narratives imparted stuck with us.

The same is true for how stories shape our understanding of different cultures, philosophies, and ways of life. When you first learned about Hinduism, Buddhism, Indigenous beliefs or any other cultures and religions, you probably encountered their core narratives and myths first. Those ancient stories pack powerful metaphors and lessons about each culture's values, beliefs about the nature of existence, and guidelines for ethical conduct.

Just look at some of the most famous and influential stories ever told across the world, from Abrahamic tales in the Bible and Quran to the Hindu Vedas and Bhagavad Gita to Aesop's fables and more. Stripping away the supernatural embellishments, at their core these ancient narratives were jam-packed with wisdom about how to live a moral, ethical, purposeful life in harmony with others and the natural world.

Contemporary stories continue shaping our understanding of the world too. Every society has its defining stories that reveal its values, hopes, fears and perspectives. American stories tend to emphasize individualism, working hard to achieve your dreams against adversity, and the struggle for freedom and justice. Recent stories from China might highlight traditions, philosophical themes around harmony and balance, or tales of sacrifice for the greater good.

Even as kids, the stories we're exposed to impart subtle lessons and assumptions about gender roles, family dynamics, good vs. evil, and so much more. The tales we absorb construct our foundational beliefs and mental frameworks about how the world works.

Beyond just their literal meanings, stories also shape abstract thoughts through symbolism, metaphor, and emotional resonance. One of my favorite examples is how J.R.R. Tolkien's Lord of the Rings legendarium delves into complex themes about the seductive nature of corrupting power, moral resilience, environmentalism, and the struggle between good and evil existing in all things. While on the surface it's just a fictional fantasy tale, it explores vital philosophical questions that have influenced many readers' broader perspectives on ethics and life itself over the decades.

Or look at how George Orwell's Animal Farm used the simple device of animal characters to symbolically expose the horrors of totalitarian oppression and corrupting ambition in a way that helped generations understand those heavy themes on a gut level. Metaphors and symbolism embedded in stories make complex truths tangible and visceral.

Stories' profound ability to move us emotionally is also a big part of how they influence our mindsets and views. When you're emotionally invested in a narrative and its characters, their journeys, beliefs and choices stick with you far more than any lecture or essay could.

You understand and empathize with different characters' diverse perspectives because you've experienced the world through their emotional lens. Their pains, struggles and joys resonate within you, shaping your own sense of reality and wisdom about the human experience in a way facts alone can't achieve.

From this internalized emotional place, the stories' deeper meanings, insights and philosophies organically influence your own internal beliefs, assumptions, and overall worldview a bit more with each impactful tale you consume. Even if the cautionary tales of sin and temptation in something like John Milton's Paradise Lost don't align with your religious views, you can't help but ruminate on the philosophical truths it explores about desire, morality and humanity's flawed condition.

Furthermore, well-crafted stories allow us to gain deeper insights into unfamiliar people, cultures and ways of thinking by letting us live experiences through different characters' eyes for a while. By exploring immigrant narratives, tales from LGBTQ+ and neurodivergent authors, or foreign fables and folklore, we're able to cultivate more empathy, open-mindedness and greater understanding of other worldviews, thought processes and lived realities that differ from our own.

Then there's how science fiction stories in particular spark imagination and questioning about the boundaries of reality, technology, morality and existence itself. What if humans could become technological beings and transcend biology? What if we made contact with alien life or discovered evidence of universe altering phenomena? How might radically advanced technologies disrupt human society, identity and consciousness? Would those things even be comprehensible to our current frameworks?

Impactful sci-fi tales don't just entertain, they nudge us to re-examine our assumptions and limitations about what's possible or understood. They expand our minds to transcend current models of existence by offering thoughtful speculation grounded in personal, relatable narratives.

At the end of the day, stories provide meaning, emotional truth and profound wisdom that raw data alone cannot fully capture about the world and our place within it. More than just entertainment, stories encode philosophies, beliefs, perspectives and revelations about reality in engaging, unforgettable ways that penetrate our psyches, shaping our consciousness and understanding from the roots up.

While we can articulate our views through analytical essays or abstract arguments, stories engage both our intellect and emotions simultaneously. Their illuminating fables, poignant character arcs and powerful symbolism become cognitive and emotional time bombs detonating new epiphanies about life, morality, society and existence itself. Thoughtful stories are ultimately a powerful, deeply impactful tool for both individuals and cultures to evolve their mindsets and perceptions as they wrestle with narrative truths beyond just the words themselves.

That's the timeless magic and value of this ancient human tradition of storytelling. Beyond mere entertainment, stories essentially construct the lenses through which we interpret and understand reality itself across all its beautiful, messy, profound and diverse manifestations throughout the human experience. They're the operative code upholding the very operating systems of our worldviews and consciousness as individuals and cultures across history.

The different types of stories (novels, movies, myths, etc.)

While we've explored how stories shape our understanding of the world and some of their deeper purposes, it's important to recognize that stories come in a crazy variety of formats and genres too. From ancient spoken myths and fables to today's literary novels, films, TV shows video games and more. Each different type of story wields its own unique strengths for enlightening and entertaining us.

Let's start with some of the earliest forms of narrative myths, legends and folktales. Before writing was even a thing, these oral traditions preserved and passed down a culture's core beliefs, histories and wisdom across generations through imaginative tales of gods, heroes, supernatural events and moral lessons. Myths like the Epic of Gilgamesh from Mesopotamia or the ancient Greek classics by Homer weren't just wild yarns, they explained things like the origins of the world, natural phenomena, and the human condition itself through symbolic narratives.

Folk tales and fables were simpler stories that used talking animals or scenarios with obvious symbolism to impart bite-sized ethical guidance on topics like hospitality, greed, perseverance and other valued virtues. Stories like Aesop's famous fables lampooning human flaws and hubris created digestible parables to get their points across in memorable ways that stuck with audiences much better than dull lectures.

As cultures advanced writing systems, poetry emerged as an artful narrative form that used vivid metaphors and evocative language to express deeper truths and emotions. From ancient Mesopotamian epics to Sanskrit Vedic verses to masterpieces like Homer's Iliad and Odyssey, poetic stories emphasized verbal craftsmanship and creative expression as vessels for profundity about the world.

Eventually, longer prose fiction narratives like novels and short stories became wildly popular with the spread of printing presses and more widespread literacy. The unrestricted creative possibilities of these extended narratives allowed authors to craft rich, complex stories capable of deeply exploring the human experience through carefully developed plots, settings, characters and themes.

Just think of profound literary novels that have profoundly shaped culture. Talking about heady topics like morality, class struggles, violence, racism, politics and the search for meaning and purpose in life. From Mary Shelley's Frankenstein delving into playing god and humanity's hubris to George Orwell's 1984 satirizing totalitarian control to Jean Toomer's Cane giving voice to the African diaspora experience to Toni Morrison's gut-wrenching stories about the Black experience in America and so many more examples. Novels uniquely excel at immersing us in thought provoking, transformative narratives on an intellectual and emotional level.

With the rise of relatively new mediums like cinema in the 20th century, visual storytelling in films and TV shows exploded in popularity. While drawing inspiration from theater and literature, these narrative forms merged visual artistry and dynamic camerawork with immersive world building, sound design, performance, editing rhythms, and more to bring enthralling stories to life unlike ever before.

Not only could they adapt beloved novels and historical tales to the screen, but entirely new types of stories customized for the strengths of each visual medium flourished too. From bombastic spectacles emphasizing jaw-dropping action and visuals to gritty, intimate character studies depicting the human condition with raw power unique to the film/TV medium.

Today's cutting-edge interactive video games meanwhile merge traditional scripted narratives with player agency, embodied POV (Point Of View) and dynamic systems where your choices can radically alter the trajectory of the story you experience. These games are constantly pushing the boundaries of what it even means to be an active participant in a narrative rather than just a passive observer or listener. Talk about an unprecedented evolution for the ancient art of storytelling!

Of course, even as new narrative mediums and genres emerge, older forms like theatrical plays, narrative poetry, oral tales, myths, and epic verses remain timeless ways of expressing the human experience through story too. In fact, I'd argue that humanity's core drive to creatively express ourselves through narratives is a defining quality of our species. Embedded in our DNA, constantly evolving to fit new creative mediums over the eons.

But no matter the type of story we're talking about, whether ancient mythologies, Shakespearean tragedies, Victorian novels, Golden Age comic books, prestige TV dramas or eSports streamed over the internet. They all represent different creative vessels for expressing universal human truths and parsing the profound depths of the experience we all share as conscious, feeling beings fumbling our way through this bewildering existence together.

And that's really the power and magic of stories as an art form, no matter what particular style or genre we're exploring. They provide thoughtful frameworks for making sense of our cultures, psyches, relationships, the natural world, mortality, struggles, and joys. The full spectrum of what it means to be alive as humans. Mythological stories may attempt to explain the origins of the universe and natural order; historical fiction seeks enlightening perspectives into other lived experiences; sci-fi lets us ponder humanity's possible futures and reckon with potentials of transformative technologies.

Basically, every civilization and people throughout history have crafted narratives as metaphorical lenses for grappling with the Big Questions all conscious beings inevitably wrestle with: Why are we here? What's our purpose? How should we behave and treat each other? What are the boundaries of reality and cognition? What might an existence beyond our own finite lives and worlds look like?

The immense diversity of narrative forms and genres allows creative storytellers to pose these heady philosophical queries in unique ways that resonate with different individuals and cultures. Approaching that universal wellspring of human wisdom, experience and profundity. From myriad thematic angles and creative visions. That's the essence of storytelling's enduring value and importance across time, societies and modes of expression.

Whether it's parables about moral conduct embedded in ancient fables or cutting-edge video game narratives exploring the existential implications of simulated realities, human beings simply cannot help but clothe our driving questions and beliefs about reality itself within the familiar frameworks of stories and characters. It's a primal creative urge that has united our species since the dawn of consciousness. To understand ourselves and existence through the revelatory lens of imaginative narratives that synthesize information into emotional truths.

So while the mediums and genres continue evolving rapidly in our ever-accelerating world, that core purpose of stories remains constant. Creatively expressing our shared human struggles, beliefs, hopes, fears and philosophies about reality. Through engaging tales that capture both intellect and spirit. Stories unite us by illuminating our universally profound, messy and wonderful experience of simply being alive in this strange cosmos. They record our journey across generations as we organically evolve new myths and narratives to continually re-contextualize our fleeting existence into meaningful universal truths.

Chapter 2: The Anatomy of a Story

The essential elements of a story (characters, plot, conflict, etc.)
Every memorable story ever told, no matter how unique or groundbreaking, is built from the same fundamental building blocks. These core story elements form the basic anatomy underlying all narratives, from ancient myths and fairy tales to contemporary literary classics and blockbuster movies.

Once you understand the essential components like character, plot, conflict, and theme that make up the skeletal framework for crafting engaging stories, you'll gain powerful insights into how these forces intertwine to produce those magical, emotionally resonant experiences that leave an indelible mark on your imagination and soul.

So let's dive into breaking down the nuts and bolts of what creates a truly impactful, well-structured narrative:

Characters at the heart of every tale, no matter how wild the escapist fantasy or mind-bending the subject matter, compelling characters are your anchor for forging emotional connections with your audience. These represented personas, whether fictional or based on real figures, cultivate the empathetic bonds that make us invest in their struggles, celebrate their triumphs, and ultimately embrace the deeper thematic messaging their arcs are expressing.

To create characters that resonate, you need multidimensional personas exhibiting authentic human depth and complexity through their personalities, backgrounds, flaws, desires and psychological motivations driving their actions. The most memorable protagonists, like Hamlet or Katniss Everdeen, are imbued with such nuanced inner lives and agency that their narratives become modern mythic reflections of the breadth of human consciousness and willpower.

Of course, memorable tales don't just require one iconic lead, they need an ensemble of well-developed characters bouncing off one another with distinctly clashing personalities, agendas and roles to propel the escalating tensions and interweaving subplots onward. From the hero's trusty sidekick and cunning mentor figures to imposing villains personifying evil and seductive temptations, these dynamic character interplays spawn the riveting high-stakes moments that cement themselves into our cultural psyches.

Plot

If characters represent the emotional heartbeats of a narrative experience, then plot provides the pumping circulatory system to propel that heart forward on its eventful journey. At its core, a plot maps the causal sequence of scenes depicting the characters' actions and complications driving the narrative's escalating momentum. It's the delicately choreographed series of events continually ratcheting up the narrative tension and high stakes that hook audiences at a cerebral, thematic level.

The most resonant plots aren't just relentless thrill-rides though, they're purposefully structured from setups and payoffs to imbue the journey's twists and turns with deep symbolic significance. Each high point, reversal and narrative beat represents an intentional story beat communicating profound observations about the human condition underlying the surface-level action and spectacle.

The basic skeletal frameworks like the Three-Act Structure or the mythological Monmouth cycle outline these carefully modulated ebbs and flows to deliver maximum thematic impact. As the hero cycles through the distinct stages, from an enticing hook introducing their world, through an escalating series of obstacles and ordeals leaving them permanently transformed, to a rousing climactic triumph resolving the central driving question or conflict, these deeply ingrained narrative patterns mirror and illuminate the archetypal stages and transformations of the human experience itself.

Conflict, you can't have a compelling plot without formidable conflicts continually driving it forward and raising the dramatic stakes, now can you? Conflict, stemming from clashing desires, ethical dilemmas, or oppositional forces, quite literally births narrative momentum by forcing the protagonist to wrestle with substantive challenges that create ample opportunities for character growth, thematic exploration and high-stakes tensions to engage audiences.

On the surface, these conflicts can manifest as physical external struggles like the hero battling a tangible villain, overcoming daunting trials like war or natural disasters, or journeying through dangerous realms. However, the most memorable tales don't just dwell on surface-level thrills; they use these external conflicts as self-reflective mirrors to also probe the internal psychological and emotional turmoil plaguing their characters.

Did the hero forsake their virtuous identity and moral code while defeating the nefarious villain? Did they succumb to the tantalizing temptation dangled before them, only to reap disastrous consequences? These inner emotional and existential conflicts experienced by characters are the true heart that elevates gripping narratives into timeless human meditations on desire, identity, ethics, spirituality and more. They crystallize allegorical wisdom into potent parables that stick with us long after the literal plot details fade from memory.

Theme, while unforgettable characters, engrossing plots and escalating conflicts build the addictive forward narrative momentum keeping audiences voraciously consuming your tale, it's the deeper thematic meanings explored through these elements that ultimately determines your story's lingering emotional resonance and philosophical impact.

Theme represents the core ideas, insights and subjective truths you're using the narrative's events, character arcs and symbolic subtext to communicate underlying subject matter and existential meditations on the human condition. In other words, theme is the payload of resonant truth and wisdom your story transports into readers' minds and hearts, potentially shifting their perceptions about themselves and reality itself, that's what elevates a story into a revelatory experience transcending mere ephemeral entertainment.

For instance, under the surface thrills of a mythic fantasy epic evoking the Monmouth cycle like Lord of the Rings, the story imparts profound themes about addiction to corrupting power, moral perseverance against totalitarian evil, the resilience of the environmental push against industrial blight, and even archetypal musings on embracing death as a catalyst for regeneration. While framed through imaginative events in a fictional realm, these symbolic narrative threads directly illuminate perennial philosophical queries about ethics, morality, society and the cyclical patterns of existence that have archetypal resonance for human civilizations across history.

A truly great story isn't simply feeding you a passive experience, it's indelibly altering your consciousness and framing new perspectives by harmonizing its imagistic narrative elements into overarching symbolic arias articulating fundamental human truths that trigger those indelible "Aha!" moments of clarity and transcendent epiphany. That sublime impact is the mark of how storytelling has functioned as a reverberating trans-generational conduit for cultures to pass down their most vital existential wisdom, ethics and defining community identities since the dawn of human mythologies.

So in summary, no matter how you approach constructing a great narrative, whether building from archetypal character foundations, meticulously plotting out a tightly woven causal sequence of escalating tensions, choreographing iconic internal and external conflicts to force protagonists into their hero's journey transformations, or exploring specific themes and philosophical messaging - you're engaging with the fundamental molecular building blocks that collectively form the universal DNA of what composes a deeply resonant story experience. Master these core elements, understand their interwoven connections, and you'll wield the keys to conjuring narrative experiences capable of transporting minds, touching souls, and ultimately imparting some profound wisdom about our grand human odyssey transpiring across this strange universe.

The difference between story and narrative.

You've probably heard the terms "story" and "narrative" used almost interchangeably when talking about books, movies, TV shows and other entertainment. But while they're definitely related concepts, there are some key distinctions between story and narrative that are important to understand as a storyteller.

At their core, a story refers to the basic sequence of events or plotline depicting a character or group of characters journeying through a series of struggles, obstacles and conflicts working towards an eventual resolution or conclusion. It's essentially the chronological through-line of the "what happens" in a particular tale.

For example, the basic story of *Star Wars: A New Hope* boils down to: Luke Skywalker joins the Rebel Alliance, gets trained to become a Jedi, helps destroy the Empire's Death Star battle station after his friends are threatened. That's the barebones chain of major events and actions advancing the story's plot from beginning to end in that movie.

A narrative, on the other hand, involves the actual craft of purposefully constructing, ordering and presenting those story events through an intentional perspective and framework to deliver a specific experience for the audience absorbing the tale.

In the case of *Star Wars*, the narrative delivery involves introducing Luke as a restless youth living a humble life on the planet, Tatooine, receiving a cosmic calling from the old Jeti Obi-Wan, assembling a ragtag crew of allies, experiencing setbacks and casualties along the journey, facing trials that force him to embrace his latent powers and finally triumphing in a climactic battle that destroys the Empire's terrifying ultimate weapon. This precise sequencing and contextualization of the events into evocative setups, complications, and pay-offs, along with things like character arcs, world building details, dialogue, and escalating stakes, that's what defines the overarching narrative encapsulating the story's raw events.

So in essence, a story represents the chronological backbone or "what happened", while a narrative signifies the tactical delivery mechanisms like selective framing, emphasis, and context-shaping used to most optimally immerse audiences within that story experience. Basically, every story gets filtered through an intentional narrative voice, style and presentation strategy when crafted into an actual final creative experience for consumption.

Applying this to your favorite books or films, you can separate the core story events from the purposeful narrative frameworks constructing and presenting those events in specific ways. The story of *Hamlet* involves a prince uncovering his father's murderer and wrestling with whether to enact revenge, climaxing in a bloodbath resolving that central conflict. However, the actual narrative presentation of that story in Shakespeare's famous play involves carefully shaping elements like:

- Introducing Hamlet through the foreboding supernatural visitation of his father's ghost crying out for vengeance to establish an ominous tone and frame Hamlet's inner torment over his colossal call to action
- Populating the tale with a rich ensemble of well-drawn characters like Ophelia, Claudius, Gertrude and more who both amplify the central conflicts while personifying various ideas, ethical quandaries and psychological tensions underpinning Hamlet's struggles in nuanced ways
- Layering the language, settings, motifs and plot developments with dense symbolic subtext exploring

complex existential themes about morality, the virtue of violence, toxic masculinity, the human condition and much more
- Employing theatrical devices like dramatic speeches, asides to the audience, witty wordplay, ironic cosmic jokes by the universe and more to modulate the storytelling experience with metatextual depth
- Delaying the central revenge plot's final resolution with compelling detours complicating Hamlet's motivations and psychological Catch-22s he must navigate

So while the basic story focuses on the linear sequence of Hamlet avenging his father's murder, the actual narrative framework Shakespeare employed goes far beyond just depicting those basic events. By purposefully choreographing the story events through a nuanced, symbolic, psychologically-rich, tonally ominous and metatextual layered delivery system, the resulting finalized narrative work elevates the tale into a profound meditation on spirituality, ethics, madness and the spectrum of human experiences that lingers with audiences on a deeper thematic level.

This delineation between story and narrative becomes even more amplified when analyzing more experimental, avant-garde or non-linear narratives that deconstruct traditional storytelling conventions. For instance, in the cult classic *Pulp Fiction*, the story's events ultimately follow a chronological order of:

Jules and Vincent retrieve a mystery suitcase, encounter some crazy s***, then Jules decides to change his path in life. Butch double-crosses some gangsters, flees the city, returns to get his watch and accidentally saves the gangsters' lives instead. Vincent inadvertently kills someone and tries covering it up with Jules.

However, the actual narrative's non-linear structure presents those story events in a remixed, out-of-order sequence, repeatedly circling back upon different characters and timeline fragments through an anthology style approach filled with tangents, talkative character detours, and even a metatextual sequence depicting the creation of the story itself being narrated.

So in *Pulp Fiction*, while the story's true beginning-to-end chain of events can eventually be parsed out, the purposefully fractured, anachronistic and metatextual narrative presentation cloaks the tale in multiple abstractions. This enhances the surreal, noir-pulp vibe and themes of chaos theory undergirding the entire experience by scrambling the traditional delivery mechanics of how stories are typically depicted in digestible beginning-middle-end progressions.

Across formats like movies, TV, novels, plays, video games and more, narratives employ all sorts of clever framing devices, subversions, and remixing shenanigans to modulate how the core story information is ultimately conveyed to audiences. And that's where so much of a narrative's distinctive creative value emerges, in the purposeful arranging, pacing, contextualization and stylization elevating a raw story into an artful, resonant experience provoking thoughtful reactions and analyzing existence itself through the kaleidoscopic filters of diverse lenses.

At the end of the day, while a story simply outlines the chronological backbone of events, a narrative adds creative intentionality and purpose in how those series of moments are packaged into a cohesive artistic experience. The story forms the penciled skeleton, while the narrative manifests the intricate musculature, textures and dynamic choreography bringing that skeletal framework pulsing to life in the specific ways the creators envision for maximum thematic and emotional impact on audiences.

So the next time you dive into a new narrative experience in whichever medium, see if you can identify both the core story's events and how the purposeful narrative decisions enhance your experience of absorbing that story's deeper wisdom and truths. I guarantee you'll start appreciating the levels of authorial craftsmanship and creativity embedded in your favorite stories in a whole new light!

The Three-Act Structure and Other Story Frameworks.

One of the most crucial skills for any storyteller to master is understanding the fundamental story structure frameworks that have formed the architectural blueprints for crafting cohesive, engaging narrative experiences across cultures and mediums for centuries.

While there are a variety of different structural paradigms out there, they all follow a consistent set of universal principles about how to optimally sequence and develop the core dramatic elements like character arcs, rising tensions, narrative stakes and thematic explorations into a holistic, emotionally satisfying experience for audiences.

The most well-known and widely-utilized model is the *Three-Act Structure*, which maps out storytelling into an intuitive beginning, middle and end progression. Let's break down how this time-tested structure functions as the skeletal framework many narratives follow:

Act 1: The Setup This opening act establishes the story's core characters, their surrounding world and the "status quo" of their circumstances before the disruption propelling everything into motion. We meet the protagonist living within their baseline normal reality, get insights into their back stories and personalities, and glimpse their conscious and unconscious wants/needs that will eventually thrust them into action once the main conflict emerges.

Importantly, Act 1 also firmly "plants the seeds" that will blossom throughout the rest of the story, laying down subtle foreshadowing hints and Chekhov's gun details that may initially seem trivial but will pay off as harbingers of the much larger dramatic arcs, symbolic motifs and narrative developments to come later on. This careful setup work creates cohesion and subconscious emotional investments that satisfy audiences.

By the end of this opening act, something happens to disrupt the established status quo, an instigating incident intrudes that the protagonist initially resists but will eventually be forced to confront head-on. This critical, clearly defined inciting incident sparks the character's central motivation or call-to-adventure that rockets the story momentum into Act 2.

Act 2: Confrontation The vast middle section of most stories, Act 2 represents an escalating upward trajectory continually raising the dramatic stakes and narrative tensions through increasingly complicated obstacles and higher-risk dilemmas the protagonist must navigate.

After crossing the point of no return into embarking on their central journey or mission, the characters encounter a series of new character introductions, subplots, unexpected developments and reversals that progressively push them towards a metaphorical or literal threshold they must traverse at the end of this act.

These narrative complications all build upon the threads and setups established in Act 1, allowing ample time for complex character arcs, nuanced thematic explorations, and steadily intensifying conflicts to manifest at an escalating rate heading towards an inevitable climactic confrontation or point of utmost risk and renewal for the protagonist.

The most resonant Act 2 sequences immerse audiences in rich world building and introduce increasingly formidable antagonistic forces that personify and crystallize the dramatic dilemmas / thematic messaging underpinning the entire story's reason for existing. These tantalizing narrative crumbs entice viewers to theorize where things could be headed while slowly deconstructing the protagonist's old belief systems, relationships or circumstances before transitioning into the transformational final act.

Act 3: Resolution, this climactic act finally reaches thedramatic breaking point following the steadily accumulating narrative momentum. The protagonist must confront the story's central conflict forces head-on, undergoing a profound transformational arc before achieving some hard-won decisive resolution determining whether they either achieve or fail to attain their goals.

If written compellingly, the buildup of dramatic anticipation keeps viewers riveted during these harrowing critical junctures as the protagonist navigates the existential gauntlet. Mastering the art of dramatic pacing and raising the narrative stakes to an emotional fever pitch prior to this ultimate conflict is key for achieving catharsis and resonance.

After this dramatic confrontation peaked by all the character development and subtext seeded in the previous acts, the story enters its denouement bridging towards a finalized resolution before the closing credits or chapter. Here the audience gains closure on any remaining loose threads and clearly comprehends the final lessons or meaning imparted by the protagonist's journey, whether triumphing against all odds or being undone by irresolvable flaws or forces larger than themselves.

This basic *Three-Act Structure* forms the fundamental blueprint from which most storytellers craft their tale's overall foundations and dramatic pacing. From Shakespeare's tragedies and classic Hollywood films to novel trilogies, the defined acts provide familiar modular narrative touchstones for hooking audience investment, escalating tensions, delivering cathartic resolutions and wrapping up philosophical completeness by the end.

Of course, many other structural storytelling frameworks flesh out and expand upon this core three-act paradigm with additional nuanced stages to follow, such as introducing distinct stage like the "Approach to the Inmost Cave" or "Resurrection" phases found within Joseph Campbell's celebrated "Hero's Journey" mythological blueprint.

The Hero's Journey essentially maps out a full cyclical reincarnation loop tracking how an ordinary individual gets whisked away from their mundane daily lives into an unknown metaphysical realm. There they must undergo increasingly difficult tests and confront metaphoric demons representing their deepest fears, ultimately attaining some profound transformation before returning as a reborn allegorical savior to their old world now centered by the expanded perspectives gained.

Other structural frameworks prioritize specific cultural storytelling traditions, like the *Five-Act Structure* prevalent in Indian epics subdividing the action into more granular phases including an Opening/Introduction phase, the Germ/Catalytic subdivision where the central conflict emerges, the Rising Action continually intensifying complications, the Tragic Note/Climax where the narrative reaches peak upheaval and a Falling Action/Catastrophe finale culminating the dramatic resolution.

Regardless which specific framework you follow, the core underlying principle remains the same, to effectively modulate dramatic escalation, rising and falling tension patterns, character evolutions, and profound thematic explorations following an intentional architecture conducive for hooking audience engagement, sustaining viewer interests, and achieving an emotionally resonant final payoff simultaneously enlightening and entertaining.

When crafting a great story experience, you must consider both the underlying chronological story events themselves, but also how you can strategically arrange and present that information through the familiar yet flexible frameworks that have endured for so long precisely because their principles for dramatic pacing and progression align with the intrinsic ways our pattern-seeking human psyches naturally crave narratives to resolve into enlightening epiphanies and poignant transformative experiences reflecting our shared existence.

So whether adhering faithfully to the three-act playbook or experimenting with remixing and hybridizing elements from various other frameworks, understanding these foundational structural blueprints unlocks revelatory powers for creating profoundly memorable and impactful narrative experiences that linger in your audiences' consciousness forevermore.

Chapter 3: Creating Compelling Characters

The importance of well-developed characters

Want to know the single most important element for crafting a truly great, emotionally resonant story that sticks with audiences long after the credits roll or that final page gets turned? It's creating nuanced, psychologically authentic characters who feel like fully fleshed-out human beings.

Think about it, we've all had that experience of being utterly transfixed watching a pretty lackluster movie or reading a seemingly formulaic book simply because the characters leapt off the screen or page as vibrantly alive individuals we desperately cared about and empathized with on a deep, emotional level.

On the flip side, you've also likely slogged through critically-acclaimed films or literary novels boasting brilliant cinematography and prose only to find the thinly-sketched protagonists so one-dimensional and devoid of interiority that you simply couldn't work up any emotional investment in their arcs or the story's messaging as a result.

At the end of the day, great stories live or die not by their wildly inventive high concepts, crackling suspense, or thought-provoking themes alone, but by the resonance of their characters' humanity. It's the richly realized personalities exhibiting authentic quirks, ambiguities and emotional depths reflecting our own muddled experiences as flawed people trying to find purpose amidst this crazy world that ultimately make us obsessively consume certain narratives over and over again.

Which brings me to the core importance of devoting serious creative energy into constructing multidimensional, psychologically cohesive character foundations as the entry point for any tale you hope will truly endure and enlighten your audiences. Because no matter how ingenious your narrative's broader dramatic through lines and structural architecture may be, the audience's solitary conduit for absorbing that messaging comes via the identifiable personas embodying the underlying human truths you're trying to impart through imaginative storytelling in the first place.

The most transcendent literary classics, like Tolstoy's *Anna Karenina* or Harper Lee's *To Kill a Mockingbird*, are revered not just for their symbolic cultural significance and matchless descriptive prose, it's that the central characters of Anna, Levin, Scout, Atticus and Boo Radley exist as such stunningly complete reflections of the full breadth of the human experience. Their interior thoughts, philosophical quandaries, personality contradictions and overarching thematic arcs illustrate inescapable existential reckonings we all must navigate as conscious individuals, from confronting societal prejudices and moral ethical hypocrisies to questioning our cosmic purpose in a seemingly indifferent universe.

The same principles apply to any and all narrative formats, whether you're looking at modern masterpieces of television like *Breaking Bad*, *The Wire* or *The Leftovers*, unskippable gaming narratives like *The Last of Us* exploring found-family relationships amidst apocalyptic bleakness, or paradigm-shattering works of cinematic transcendence like Charlie Kaufman's *Synecdoche, New York* and its profound meditation on the very nature of human consciousness itself. In each instance, the key entry point forging that indelible connection cementing these stories into the cultural zeitgeist comes through their uncompromising commitment to probing the myriad complexities of the represented personas caught within their dramatic crucibles.

Even the most superficially thrilling or escapist stories centered around action-packed spectacle or mind-bending speculative fiction only maintain lasting relevance because of the audiences' parasocial bonding experiences with the meticulously constructed identities embodying those worlds and imaginative conceits. It's hard to imagine the original *Star Wars* saga's archetypal narrative vessels of Luke, Leia, Vader and Han Solo achieving generationally resonating myth status without so much emotional bandwidth invested in their grounded yet iconic characterizations. Each represents a facet of our own inner conflicts between selfishness and sacrifice, destiny and free will.

The same philosophy extends to more fantastical creations like Gandalf from *The Lord of the Rings* books or Walter White from the *Breaking Bad* saga their larger-than-life personas still register as profoundly real because each exhibits richly-layered moral complexities, messy human contradictions and transformational identity arcs emblematic of the turbulence echoing through all our existential journeys as flawed individuals seeking purpose. Deep down, these characters resonating across innumerable stories tap into intrinsically recognizable wellsprings reflecting our own contradictory unconscious yearnings, unspeakable shames and heroic strivings for self-actualization.

So whether you're conceiving a gritty crime character study rooted in unflinching realism or conjuring a larger-than-life fantasy hero destined to reverberate as a modern mythological emblem, the key creative starting point remains studiously plumbing the depths of that character's psyche and inner being to imbue them with staggering verisimilitude as a complete human entity striving against their individual crucibles of suffering, doubt and striving for meaning. Only by following that fundamentally empathic creative pathway can your constructed personas transcend one-dimensional ciphers existing merely as functional instruments to instead embodying profound subjective emotional experiences and symbolic philosophical resonances tapping into the universal human condition.

Without richly interwoven psychological substantiation, even the most meticulously developed larger-than-life presences feel lacking in the fundamental authenticity audience's subconsciouses implicitly require to stir real cathartic emotional investment. Think about iconic pop culture figures like Batman, Indiana Jones or James Bond, while deliciously entertaining within their respective fantastic conceits, the inability to comprehensively grasp their core underlying motivations, fears, belief systems and vulnerabilities is ultimately what prevents them from cohering into paradigm-shifting transcendent character bastions burrowing deep into the archetypal human psyche.

In contrast, the most emotionally transformative and enduring protagonists across storytelling canons are the ones allowing audiences to gaze unflinchingly through the opened window of their souls onto our own tortured, aspirational and triumphant experiences as existentially frustrated yet resilient inhabitants of this bizarre shared dream we call existence. They're the literary and dramatic equals injecting nuanced ambiguities and probing self-reflection into the two-dimensional archetypes embroidered into our cultural fabrics.

So as you endeavor to create the next classic protagonist reverberating across the epochs, always start from a position of crafting authentically lived-in identities we can't help but embrace as proxies for processing our own existential rollercoasters. Only through mastering the art of fully developing multidimensional characters with uniquely distinctive yet profoundly relatable interior mirrors of the human experience will your creative narrative visions and thematic insights ignite the transformative epiphanies ringing out long after each spellbinding story finally concludes.

Character archetypes and how to avoid clichés

One of the trickiest balancing acts you'll need to pull off as a storyteller is walking the delicate line between leveraging the familiarity and narrative shorthand of established character archetypes to anchor your story, while simultaneously avoiding the dreaded clichés and one-dimensional character crutches that can instantly sink your tale into eye-rolling predictability.

Because here's the tough truth, whether you like it or not, pretty much every memorable character in any enduring story ultimately boils down to an archetypal foundation that's been ingrained into the cultural narrative tradition for generations, if not centuries. Heck, even the freshest, most subversive portrayals wind up simply remixing or reimagining the tried-and-true archetypes seeded into our collective human psyches since time immemorial.

At their core, the key archetypes encompass primary character types like The Hero, The Sidekick, The Mentor, The Villain, The Love Interest, and so on. But beyond that surface categorization, their underlying archetypal traits and roles often intersect and overlap within the winding fictional journey each must undergo. This makes the true magic of memorable characterization ultimately emerge from how ingeniously writers and creators breathe nuanced, distinctive flourishes into these primordial character foundations.

That way their deeper mythological resonances still shine through in recognizable ways, sparking the audience's intrinsic "aha!" emotional payoffs that our brains latch onto. Yet the fresh metaphorical packaging and thematic allegories developed along those archetypal through lines illuminate new perspectives about ourselves and existence.

Let's look at some classic examples analyzing how the interplay of archetypal familiarity and postmodern remixing coalesces in iconic tales:

STAR WARS- The archetypal framework looks ripped straight from the Joseph Campbell playbook, with the archetypal farm boy-turned-heroic-savior mythology and inevitable rise to cosmic power, buoyed by an expansive arc evoking archetypal resonances from myth. But the fresh twist is grounding it in an endearing galactic folk tale setting, and Luke's unshakable decency sets him apart from traditional antihero alignments. This modernizes familiar archetypes through the power of nuanced personality and narrative style.

THE DARK KNIGHT- The quintessential Batman archetype channels the vigilante and protector archetypes through brooding, grounded urban Gothic tone. But the real substance emerges from Nolan weaving in timely post-9/11 relevance around the philosophy behind establishing order amidst everyday human savagery and using Batman's mythical persona to explore our lust for authoritarian strongmen saving us from our own moral frailties.

MAD MAX: FURY ROAD- A wild post-apocalyptic remix of the archetypal Loner and Warrior archetypes, blending elemental anxieties around environmental cataclysm and toxic patriarchal power structures into one euphoric existential rebellion narrative. The road warrior's endless quest for survival purpose gets radically re-energized through entanglement with Furiosa's archetypal Wayfarer's tale and explosive gender empowerment themes.

So with that context establishing how walking the archetypal tightrope works, let's look at some specific archetype frameworks that have proven repeatedly effective at resonating with audiences:

THE HERO'S JOURNEY: This is the quintessential mythological template for structuring an adventure narrative, tapping into the universal human storytelling DNA embedded in our collective unconscious. It traces the arcs of characters like Luke or Frodo as archetypal "heroes" cycling from their humdrum origins through the call to adventure, encountering supernatural guides/mentors, entering the inmost cave/underworld, enduring tests and tribulations, achieving some transformational apotheosis, and ultimately returning to their previous world having attained wisdom to heroically resolve or transcend the story's core dramatic conflict and emotional stakes.

THE HERO/OUTSIDER SAVIOR: This modern archetype taps into contemporary anxieties, depicting an unlikely, unassuming protagonist thrust into circumstances beyond their control. But as the solitary individual blessed with clarifying vision, they are uniquely positioned to heroically expose grander surrounding deceptions and save their imperiled community. Think characters from *Fight Club, The Matrix, The Hunger Games*, etc.

THE BYRONIC ANTI-HERO: For more cynically-tinged dramatic character studies, the "flawed""protagonist navigating moral ambiguities and their own worst impulses provides a rich archetype for exploring psychology, ethics, and what it means to live by one's own code. Characters like *Walter White, Dexter, The Punisher and V for Vendetta's Guy Fawkes* riff exemplify the nuances of this antihero narrative approach.

THE FOOL/TRICKSTER: This archetype is the shaker of conventions, the questioner of sacred truths, the underestimated truth-teller whose mischievous wiles and seeming innocuous facade masks biting satire and potent examinations of social norms. Classic examples include Shakespearean fools, characters like Benjamin from *The Catcher in the Rye* or Tyler Durden from *Fight Club* - disruptive figures who reveal our human frailties through their madcap antics.

THE CAREGIVER/MENTOR: Typically, a supportive older figure providing the protagonist with guidance and tough love while exemplifying human qualities like compassion and wisdom, the Mentor helps the hero navigate their character journey. Think Atticus Finch from *To Kill a Mockingbird* or Gandalf from *Lord of the Rings*.

So, while I could delve into more archetypes like The Warrior, The Underdog, The Sacrifice and so on, you get the idea. Every great character is a canvas where familiar thematic threads and primal motivations are realistically colored while still retaining those universally resonant archetypal foundations.

Essentially, it's about aligning characters' symbolic journeys and fundamental human experiences with their archetypal mythological underpinnings for relatability, while constantly innovating with believability, nuance and allegories relevant to your unique perspective and theme. That's how you avoid narrative clichés. Not by endlessly discarding archetypes, but by creatively customizing them to forge your own identifiable truth within those mythological frameworks.

So don't simply rehash tired old archetypes note-for-note, but also don't toss them aside entirely, those archetypal DNA strands provide a sturdy backbone that you renovate into bold new revelations about the human experience. Because as unique as your characters and stories may be, ultimately they'll resonate most profoundly precisely because of how skillfully they tap into those timeless archetypal resonances echoing through humanity's oldest stories while revitalizing them with a fresh, singular voice.

Techniques for revealing character through action and dialogue.

One of the most common pitfalls for writers trying to create compelling, nuanced characters is relying too heavily on just straightforward exposition and internal monologues to communicate their personalities and inner struggles. While those techniques can prove effective in moderation, nothing quite brings a fictional persona to vivid life like revelatory actions and dialogue that show rather than merely tell the audience who this character fundamentally is.

The old adage of "writing is rewriting" especially applies to this aspect of characterization. Your initial drafts might feature more explicit internal narration articulating a character's background details, emotional mindsets and thematic functionality. But the revision process should focus on translating and condensing those descriptive essences into immersive, lived-in experiential moments and conversational interactions amplifying the authenticity.

Let's look at some specific techniques for using action and dialogue to build characters into fully-realized identities resonating with truth:

Physicality and Mannerisms when first introduced to a character, their physical appearance and behaviorisms provide those instantaneous unspoken insights into their underlying persona even before dialogue kicks in. Subtle details like a cautious sideways glance, an impatient foot-tapping, a pursed lip pause before replying, these all activate the audience's intuitive ability to extrapolate entire psychological portraits from sparse observational cues.

Maybe your character sports worn, threadbare clothing signaling an impoverished background without needing exposition. A lanky, loping stride could hint at an awkward adolescence, while restless hands fidgeting with any nearby objects might visually communicate an abundance of nervous tics. A character's gait, posture, seemingly unconscious habits and physical quirks can convey volumes about their demeanor, temperament and inner psyche without a single line of dialogue.

Beyond visual mannerisms, consider auditory ones too. Does your character speak with an accent that connotes a specific regional upbringing? Do they punctuate sentences with ponderous "umms" and "ahhs", indicative of a shy, calculating personality? Or perhaps their voice booms through any room, suggesting an inherently authoritative or extroverted presence.

The key is peppering in these specific idiosyncratic physical and auditory details throughout your action descriptions to create that immediate visceral familiarity between audience and character long before any overt exposition kicks in. I'm talking about techniques like: "She nibbled at the inside of her cheek as her eyes anxiously scanned the room." Or, "When nobody replied after a long pause, he slumped back in exasperation, his meaty hand dragging down across his furrowed brow." These behavioral snapshots efficiently portray fleshed-out identities in a few deft details priming the audience's imagination.

Remember, the most memorable characters feel multidimensional because the writers focused less on simplistic labels like "loud and tough" or "brooding introvert" and more on meticulously choreographing their specific physicality to paint evocative embodied pictures conveying that essence from the outside in.

Evocative Action Sequences

Look at any iconic action set-piece from your favorite film franchises, whether a globetrotting mission in a Bond flick or one of The Raid's ferocious hallway battles. These sequences often rank among the most memorable character-defining moments precisely because of how they viscerally translate a protagonist's state-of-being into raw kinetic expression.

Luke dismantling the Death Star's exhaust vent transcends a mere action climax to become the symbolic culmination of his commitment to embracing the Force and heroic destiny. Meanwhile, Jackie Chan's most revered stunts aren't just mindless spectacles, they're entertaining embodiments of his signature resilient charisma and hard-nosed work ethic being enacted amid the choreography itself.

So when plotting out your seminal action sequences, view them not just as fleeting adrenaline spikes, but as opportunities to communicate foundational character insights through thoughtful context and choreography rather than rote mechanics. Details like a character panicking under pressure, displaying dexterous improvisation, utilizing signature weapon styles, inflicting excessive force, or exhibiting noticeable moral compunctions all convey their psychology through catalytic moments of truth.

Even outside of traditional "action" sequences per se, any decisively rendered character choices enacted through physical actions rather than expository reflection allows the audience to intuit their true motivations, ethics and core identity. We learn more about Luke Skywalker's fundamental courage and honor when he vehemently rebuffs Vader's entreaties to join the Dark Side through actions rather than hollow declamations.

Revelatory Dialogue Exchanges

While character actions undoubtedly illuminate invisible swaths about their underlying essence, the spoken word wields its own power for unveiling authentic persona insights through context, voice and conversational dynamics. The most iconic characterizations become indelible through mastery of revelatory dialogue packing immense psychological resonance into succinct interchanges.

Like great action sequences, pivotal dialogue scenes provide opportunities for conveying persona-defining crucibles where a character's deepest impulses and unconscious beliefs can leak out. Their word choices, diction patterns, emotional candor versus obfuscation, even a loaded pause can conspire to unveil their earnest feelings on issues like morality, identity, relationships and other core humanistic themes.

Iconic exchanges become indelible touchstones expressing one note of an entire philosophical aria about the human condition - think about how a few terse sentences in the "Tears in Rain" soliloquy from Blade Runner encompasses multitudes about mortality, sentience and what it means to be truly conscious. Or the raw vulnerability radiating through Michael Corleone's soul-baring confessional to his wife Kay packing a character's entire tragic arc into one compact emotional detonation.

Characters perhaps reveal their truest selves not through grandiose monologuing, but through the seemingly mundane conversational rhythms populating low-key interstitial exchanges with tertiary personalities that unveil glimpses into their psychologies through little slips of banter, momentary defensiveness, or throwaway quips. The quick, almost imperceptible evasions and deflections of quotidian conversations can communicate just as much about their insecurities and defense mechanisms.

Then you have highly-stylized instances where dialogue becomes a symbolic microcosm for power dynamics, thematic subtext, interpersonal mind games and other psychological realities playing out with loaded undertones ringing beyond the superficial exchanges. Like in David Mamet's storytelling universe, conversations often represent a high-stakes verbal dance where the actions revealed through innocuous crosstalk and verbal tics illustrate more profound character truths than any overt exposition.

So ultimately, whether through physicality, immersive action or heightened wordplay, the most resonant characterizations come to life not from ham-fisted narratorial pontification, but through skilled revelations where the artistic portrayal of each deftly realized identity gets baked directly into the language of behavior and authentically experienced persona interactions. That's the true mark of evocative literary craftsmanship!

Chapter 4: Mastering Plot and Structure

The basics of plot (exposition, rising action, climax, falling action)

Okay, so you've got your compelling characters nailed down with rich psychological backstories and clearly defined goals driving their actions. Now it's time to construct an engaging storyline that properly showcases those personas overcoming escalating obstacles and narrative complications on their thematic journeys. This is where nailing the fundamental architectural principles of solid plot structuring really comes into play.

At its core, a plot maps out the progressive unfolding of your story's events through specific stages intended to hook audience curiosity, steadily escalate conflicts and tensions, culminate in a climactic dramatic apotheosis, and ultimately resolve any lingering storylines or thematic concerns in a satisfying denouement. Each distinct plot progression exists to both propel the narrative momentum while developing your characters in purposeful arcs aligned with your overall messaging and philosophical ideas you're exploring.

So to give you a solid framework for mapping those narrative energies, let's break down the classic plot structure paradigm into its core stages:

The Exposition

This opening section serves to establish the dramatic premises and core players comprising your tale before the central driving conflicts kick into gear. The exposition sets the scene by depicting your protagonists' baseline circumstances and routines, while peppering in crucial background details about their personalities, relationships and inner lives fueling their conscious/unconscious motivations.

You'll want to swiftly but efficiently communicate the foundational "who, what, where and when" specifics grounding the audience in your story's world, while layering in symbolic foreshadowing details hinting at larger thematic territories lying in wait. The most resonant exposition plants immersive details allowing you to eventually pay off pivotal setup moments with rewarding dramatic flourishes.

Most importantly though, the exposition really needs to crystallize an empathetic human relatability anchoring why we should invest in these characters' personal arcs as their circumstances inevitably slide towards an upheaval forcing them into escalating actions driving the main plotlines forward.

The Rising Action

Once you've sufficiently established your players and their opening circumstances, it's time to trigger that disruptive instigating incident sparking everything into kinetic forward momentum. The rising action sees your protagonists first committing to tackling the dramatically-escalating central conflicts, and subsequently encountering a series of obstacles and narrative complications introducing higher and higher personal/external stakes.

This section is all about continually ratcheting up narrative pressures through unpredictable twists, reversals of fortunes, romantic entanglements, new allies/villains getting folded into the rising tensions, and profound life-altering confrontations. Your protagonists' capacities for perseverance and resilience will get tested to their breaking points as their core philosophical beliefs and identity constructs start unraveling under the story's thematic scrutiny.

Effective rising action pivots frequently between stacking new dramatic pivots atop each other with briskly escalating pacing, while allowing resonant character-driven downbeats providing respites where your principals can process their rapidly shifting circumstances before the next upheaval hits. This steadily heightening dramatic kinesis paired with nuanced emotional interiority ultimately builds a propulsive narrative head of steam careening towards its inevitable climactic explosion.

The Climax

After steadily escalating the circumstances pushing your protagonists towards their physical, emotional and philosophical nadir, the climactic turning point represents their ultimate metaphorical or literal confrontation with the story's paramount conflicts and thematic reckonings they must either overcome or succumb to.

This is the dramatic high point where everything coalesces, the highest stakes, most extreme displays of action/spectacle, the stripping away of your characters' emotional armor and facades leaving their core selves naked to the harshest interior and external pressures. All your intricately foreshadowed Chekov's gun details and lingering subplots unravel at an accelerated pace, paying off in surprising yet narratively cohesive ways as the climax barrels towards resolution or catharsis, one way or another.

Effective climaxes take the underlying thematic ideas you've woven throughout your tale and symbolically extrapolate them into life-or-death crucibles stripping away your characters' existences down to their rawest embodied expressions. By pushing them into their most heightened physical/metaphorical slaughterhouse, you capture the essence of their souls in that intensified light, allowing the audience to experience revelatory truth through that cathartic narrative climax.

Whether it's Luke Skywalker rejecting terror by confronting his shadow in the Emperor or Michael Corleone's crime family being torn apart by corruption's bitter consequences in explosive realizations, the climax serves as the dramatic aperture burning away all artifice to expose the core human truth motivating your entire story in a blaze of resolving illumination.

The Falling Action

Ideally the climactic payoff should provide a definitive culmination satisfying the overall narrative through lines, even if certain branches remain dangling for subsequent story entries to explore. So the falling action segment follows to decompress from the whirlwind climactic paroxysms by tying up loose plot threads and emotional consequences in the climax's immediate aftermath.

For example, your protagonists may need to deal with any collateral damage caused during the climactic confrontations, including deaths of key characters or personal transformations/perspectives gained from their crucible experiences. This section allows narrative breathing room to dramatize meaningful closures while reinforcing themes via these lingering denouement plotlines.

However, even in this decompression phase, the best falling action sections still maintain a cadence of rising/falling tensions before ultimately coasting towards a finalized resolution. Mini-narrative branches can spool out from the climactic catharsis, briefly re-escalating certain conflicts or contradictions before getting knotted and allowing the larger resolution to settle into finality.

The Resolution

By this closing segment, your narrative should feel thematically and philosophically complete, with any lingering tensions or ambiguities intentionally preserved to complement the broader messaging rather than act as distracting loose threads. The dramatic central questions igniting the entire journey in the first place receive their decisive resolutions, even if mystery or speculation remains to foster enduring re-interpretations for audiences.

A resolution provides narrative closure while still leaving tantalizing interpretive possibilities to ponder. Character arcs find their cathartic destiny points, key thematic statements get solidified in metaphorical daggers chiseled in stone, and the overall momentum gracefully decelerates to allow the profundity of the experience to linger in the viewer/reader's psyche long after consuming it.

So while highly stylized nonlinear stories can adeptly restructure or re-contextualize these classic plot architecture principles, the underlying philosophies remain consistent, to sequentially rapture audience engagement through an intentionally modulated roller-coaster of rising action, climactic catharsis and denouement that transports them through a thematically cohesive emotional experience uncovering resonant existential truths about the human condition.

From prehistoric campfire mythologies to today's serialized streaming epics, that ancient art of cohesive storytelling largely persists through updated remixes of this enduring plot structural framework. Because at the end of the day, audiences may ostensibly crave spectacle and escapism through their preferred narrative vessels, yet what keeps them returning again and again are tales profoundly mirroring something elemental about their own existence back in recognizable yet enlightening new ways.

By honoring these time-tested principles for modulating dramatic narrative propulsion, you'll be able to transport viewers on that transformative emotional journey to the depths of the universal human experience in entertaining yet substantial ways. And who knows, handled with sufficient creativity and intention, you just might craft the seminal emotional truth-bombs resonating for generations as revered enduring mythology in its own right!

Plotting techniques (three-act, five-act, hero's journey)

Now that we've covered the fundamental structural basics underlying how most plot progressions flow from exposition and rising tensions towards a climactic peak before winding down to a resonant resolution, it's time to dive deeper into some of the specific plotting frameworks and techniques skilled storytellers utilize to purposefully modulate those narrative energies.

While each writer ultimately needs to internalize their own unique approach to charting out their story's backbone and hitting thematic payoffs, there are several tried-and-true paradigms providing sturdy architectural blueprints for constructing cohesive, emotionally satisfying narrative arcs. Let's take a look at three of the most prevalent and versatile ones:

The Three-Act Structure

Probably the most ubiquitous and straightforward plot paradigm out there, the *Three-Act Structure* breaks your overall story down into an easily digestible Beginning, Middle, and End progression that naturally maps onto the exposition, rising action, climax/resolution flow we discussed earlier.

The beauty of this structural simplicity lies in how effortlessly it lends itself to virtually any narrative form or genre, from ancient Shakespearean plays and Hollywood blockbusters to memoirs or TV show episodic arcs. The three-act principle instinctively patterns storylines to include a first act that establishes premise/characters, a second act continuously escalating conflicts and complicating matters, before climaxing in a third act resolving the central dramatic arcs.

While you can subdivide each of the three sections into more granular segmented acts, this broad three-part division just intuitively resonates with how our minds naturally seek out narrative cohesion and thematic completion in familiar, balanced through lines.

The only real drawback is that the three-act structure can lend itself to predictable or formulaic story execution if not implemented with ingenuity and originality to subvert conventions. So your challenge as a writer becomes breathing creative life and surprising reversals into each act's expected roles.

The Five-Act Structure

While the three-act architecture represents a fairly modern Western narrative plotting approach, the five-act dramatic structure actually extends back to the ancient Greek and the trailblazing work of legendary playwrights like Sophocles, Euripides and others working within the traditions of Ancient Greek theatrical traditions.

In a five-act paradigm, the overall plot breaks down into granular segments beginning with:

Act 1
The Exposition introducing main characters, settings, premise

Act 2
The Complicating Action sparking rising conflicts

Act 3
The Crisis escalating tensions towards a pivotal turning point

Act 4
Failing Fortunes as protagonists hit their nadir

Act 5
The Dénouement bringing a climactic resolution

As you can see, the five-act model essentially expands the three-act approach by devoting more structural real estate to amplifying the gradual narrative escalation and character arcs before reaching a true climax. This allows for more meticulous, psychologically textured plot developments examining the nuances of how protagonists persevere or succumb amid compounding pressures.

Historical examples abound, Shakespeare's tragedies like Hamlet, Macbeth and Othello are all structured along these five-act principles, with each sequential segment choreographing rising complications before that final soul-shattering fifth act culmination.

The Hero's Journey (Mythological)

While the previous two delineated paradigms provide fairly straightforward architectural schematics for plotting functional narrative arcs, the *Hero's Journey model* instead taps into the richly symbolic mythological roots of how humans have instinctively structured transformative stories since our prehistoric campfire days.

Famously outlined by Joseph Campbell's treatise analyzing common heroic arcs across different cultures, the Hero's Journey captures more metaphysical story energies aligning with an archetypal protagonist leaving their mundane world behind to undergo a symbolic rebirth facilitated by entering and navigating unfamiliar mystical realms, undergoing revelatory trials before returning reborn into their old world with transcendent wisdom.

The precise breakdown maps this cyclical journey through phases like:

The Call to Adventure Crossing the Threshold into a supernatural realm Encountering supernatural allies/guides

Undergoing an Approach and Traversing the Inmost Cave Achieving the Ordeal/Apotheosis

Experiencing Death/Rebirth through transformation Ultimately Returning home as a transcendent master

Essentially, the Hero's Journey models the deeply-rooted human mythological drive to construct enlightening stories chronicling an individual's transformative arc into becoming more than they were. This universality makes the Hero's Journey highly adaptable for all sorts of modern narratives, even if just subconsciously channeling its symbolic underpinnings.

For instance, the original *Star Wars* trilogy follows Luke Skywalker's archetypal hero's journey from the Call (R2's message from Leia) to Crossing Thresholds into galactic rebellion against the Empire and receiving tutelage from Obi-Wan/Yoda as mystical mentors. His climactic trajectory through ordeal and apotheosis is framed as destroying the Empire while confronting his own inner darkness before returning as a liberated Jedi Knight.

So while far more symbolic and thematically rich in its mythological core DNA, the Hero's Journey still embodies those fundamental principles discussed earlier, establishing a world, disrupting it, escalating conflicts towards a climactic personal reckoning for the protagonist before they emerge permanently transformed by their experiences. The key difference lies in how these archetypal plotting energies get extrapolated into symbolic realms of transcendent meaning beyond just functional plot mechanics.

These three paradigms represent only a sliver of the myriad storytelling frameworks that have crystallized over the ages, but they provide a solid conceptual overview into the supple yet intentional ways seasoned writers purposefully construct resonant narrative momentum and character arcs to maximize thematic impact.

Whether working within the crisp utilitarian efficiencies of the three-act structure for taut genre storytelling, exploring more psychologically nuanced character perspectives through a five-act modulation of tensions, or aiming to encapsulate an entire archetypal metamorphosis through the cosmic mythological lens of the Hero's Journey, always be cognizant of embedding purposeful methods to your storytelling madness!

Because at the end of the day, while your creative voice and thematic ambitions will inevitably transcend rigid formulas, structured plotting frameworks exist to provide your narrative visions with a map for transporting audiences to resonant emotional and philosophical destinations worth the journey. So embrace the opportunity to build from these time-honored traditional story architectures, then transform them into innovative revelations about the universal human truths awaiting illumination within your unique creative identity.

Using dramatic tension to drive the story forward

Want to know one of the most crucial make-or-break factors separating a boring, forgettable narrative from a gripping, unput down able page-turner audience members can't get enough of? It all comes down to mastering the art of cultivating dramatic tension that steadily ratchets up in purposeful ways throughout your storytelling.

Think about it, we've all experienced getting hooked on a new book series, TV drama or movie franchise because it masterfully doled out tantalizing narrative crumbs and escalating conflicts that left us desperate to consume the next installment and unravel the subplots barreling towards their climactic resolutions. Those deft narrative tensions creators manifested tangible dramatic propulsive forces practically demanding our attentions as insatiable audience members.

On the flip side, we've all endured that disappointing slog of a movie or book failing to spark that same electrifying narrative urgency needed to keep propelling us through the story, a lull in rising action and stagnant stakes giving us little incentive to keep emotionally investing beyond sheer obligation. Maybe the plot dragged due to inadequate foreshadowing of looming complications...or characters seemed to reactively meander without clearly motivated driving trajectories pushing the tale towards an inevitable dramatic reckoning.

The point is, stories without a consistently escalating degree of suspenseful dramatic tensions perpetually elevated towards a climactic emotional release tend to prove meandering slogs audiences quickly tune out. It doesn't matter how meticulous your worldbuilding or finely-etched your characters may be, without those irresistible narrative tugs inciting our insatiable curiosity over what cliffhanger or revelation awaits around the next corner, even the most ingenious story premises quickly stall out.

So what constitutes dramatic tension anyway? At its core, it stems from deliberately orchestrating pivotal storytelling forces in constant opposition, pitting contrasting character motivations against one another, placing insurmountable obstacles between protagonists and their goals, engulfing them in escalating high-stakes external conflicts raising the personal risks, or embedding symbolic subplots questioning their philosophic belief systems.

Essentially, tensions arise whenever you introduce pivotal narrative elements jeopardizing your protagonists' status quo circumstances and forcing them to confront destabilizing antagonistic energies disrupting their journeys in ways where inaction or complacency are no longer viable options for them. This inciting incident catalyzes the core dramatic expulsions audiences crave by locking the central players into unavoidable, intensifying trajectories fueled by oppositional narrative forces.

From there, a skilled storyteller constantly employs various dramatic tactics and plot mechanisms to steadily amplify those established tensions towards seemingly unbearable thresholds that eventually combust in cathartic climactic resolutions before decompressing back to a state of relative homeostasis, only to have new tensions resurface and reignite the entire cycle again.

These can take the form of literal bombs placed under the proverbial narrative trains, so to speak. Maybe the protagonist receives a terminal medical diagnosis forcing them to confront their mortality, turbocharging pressures on unresolved subplots. Perhaps crucial allies betray the core crew's mission due to hidden agendas, increasing risks of failure. An ominous backdrop like an encroaching solar flare or imminent environmental timebomb puts nihilistic temporal boundaries on reaching desperately sought resolutions.

Or maybe the escalating dramatic tensions take on more symbolic or psychological dimensions resonating on an allegorical wavelength beyond the literal plot machinations: Like tearing away layers of a protagonist's false identities and forcing them to reckon with who they truly are at their core. Socially, conscious narratives steadily upping their critiques of systemic oppression into a powder keg of outrage. Or overarching existential storylines pitting a character's cherished philosophical belief systems into diametric opposition with mounting ambiguous experiences destabilizing those certainties.

However manifested, all of these dynamics combine like a tightly coiled spring acquiring more and more torsional energy as the story progresses towards a seemingly inevitable point where it can no longer contain the escalating tensions, resulting in an explosive dramatic climax intended to release the audience from the sustained suspense while (hopefully) paying off emotionally and thematically.

Yet a master storyteller appreciates that this cycle of perpetually escalating dramatic tensions isn't about cheaply manufacturing disingenuous melodrama just for the sake of excitement. Rather, it's applying purposeful creative pressures and pivotal obstacles in alignment with the core character motivations, philosophical themes and high-stakes circumstances foundational to the entire tale's reason for existence in the first place.

In every exemplary story with enduring dramatic resonance, the audience can detect evident patterns of narrative tension organically emerging from protagonists' conscious desires clashing with antagonistic forces and unexpected variables complicating their paths towards the deeply personal transformations their arcs are hurtling towards. The escalation of stakes, complications and psychological gauntlets protagonists must traverse all stems from that combustible collision of what they want (or think they want) versus the destabilizing internal/external oppositions threatening to deprive them of those objectives.

This purposeful narrative tension doesn't just result in tidy didactic moralizing about virtue persevering against adversity though. From the most acclaimed dramas to modern masterpieces of literary fiction, the most resonant embodiments of escalating dramatic tensions exist to probe ambiguities about humanity's fraught relationship to attaining our desires against all chaotic cosmic opposition beyond our control.

Tragic character arcs escalate dramatic pressures through the crushing weight of inexorable malefactors like fate, death, society, moral entropy and the abyss of existential dread itself. The undeniable sinking dread accumulates through masterful tension-escalation tactics until protagonists' motivations either inevitably curdle into self-destruction or sublimate into hard-won transcendence of their deluded pursuits, all while ruminating on what it means to exist as a conscious being trapped in this mortal coil.

Other tales apply escalating dramatic tensions in a more redemptive spirit, subjecting protagonists to successive tribulations and catalytic personal/external gauntlets forcing confrontations with their innermost fears, moral failings or delusions about their self-supremacy over nature and society. These escalating tensions yank the characters through radical emotional, philosophical and material upheavals facilitating growth before the final crucible catalyzes their permanent epiphanies and transformations into enlightened states of being.

So whether upping the ante towards entropy or metamorphosis, dramatic tensions serve to strip away successive emotional/existential layers from protagonists on their thematic journeys. The escalation dynamics synergize motivations, high-stakes conflicts and subversive narrative catalyses that accrete mounting urgency and suspense for audiences. When deftly choreographed, this slow-burn ratcheting of dramatic kinetic energies crystallizes in an apogee sublime moment of cathartic thematic enlightenment following resonant climactic releases.

In other words, dramatic tension becomes the alchemic catalyst compelling both character and audience to evolve their previously constrained perspectives through a profound narrative experience. It encapsulates the entire transformative reason we tell stories in the first place, to manufacture tangible energies and pivotal friction providing a psychic combustion engine for reflecting upon aspects of the human condition not so easily rendered in mundane reality.

By purposefully escalating dramatic tensions in alignment with your core characters' motivations smashing against obstacles, internal faults and external conflicts eventually combusting all artificial societal/philosophical delusions, your narrative attains the crucial pressures teasing out illuminative transcendental moments for protagonist and audience alike. When executed deftly, that dramatic tension is what forges your artistic storytelling containers into scorching-hot delivery vectors for transporting universal truths directly into people's psyches and souls.

Chapter 5: The Art of Setting

The role of setting in storytelling
When you think about all the brilliant storytelling advice focused on crafting compelling characters and structuring unputdownable plots, it's easy for the pivotal role of setting to get overshadowed and treated as an afterthought. But here's the thing - even the most iconic character arcs and masterfully engineered narrative twists ultimately emerge from and intimately intertwine with the tangible sense of place where those tales unfold.

While protagonists may personify the philosophical ideas and emotional truths at a story's thematic core, and intricately designed plots serve as the delivery mechanisms transporting us through those sagas, the world-building foundations establishing each tale's sense of time, space, and cultural context act as the omnipresent theatrical staging where all the narrative jolts and characterological evolutions we invest in as audiences ultimately derive their undeniable atmospheric resonance.

And just like we'd be unable to fully immerse within the most masterfully performed play or virtuosic concert without the specialized physics and aesthetic intentionality's of the custom-designed staging and venue elements optimizing that experience, so too do our favorite stories depend on richly evoked environmental springboards setting the appropriate tonal personas and atmospheric identities for their narrative energies to properly flourish.

Think about some of the most unforgettable tales that have burrowed deep within the collective cultural consciousness over the generations. Could J.R.R. Tolkien's *The Lord of the Rings* trilogy exist as such a profoundly indelible exploration of environmental stewardship and the eternal cycle of good battling corrosive power if not for Middle Earth's lushly baroque world-building foundations rooting the entire saga so tangibly in a sense of historical place?

Or how about F. Scott Fitzgerald's *The Great Gatsby* as the definitive documentation of American Dreams turning to ash amidst the decadence of morally-starved privilege and spectacle society, would its cast of psychologically transfixed socialites, mobsters and aspirants land with the same resonant impact if not unfolding against the evocative Jazz Age backdrops of lavish gilded Long Island manors and seedy speakeasies exuding Art Deco spirits literally haunting the American landscape?

Or let's look more modernly at a visual medium like the acclaimed TV crime saga *The Wire*, where so much of the show's nuanced dissections of institutional suffering and marginalization within urban America derive their immersive authenticity from David Simon and team's starkly atmospheric renderings of contemporary Baltimore and its tangibility as a crumbling rust belt microcosm. Everything from the red-brick rowhome projects and dilapidated high schools to the seedy harbor districts and creaking bureaucracy offices helps subliminally locate the narratives exploring tribalism, cyclical violence and forsaken hope within that very specific modern American sense of civic identity decay.

In these regards, setting becomes far more than just a secondary stage dressing propping up surface-level aesthetics or scene transitions for character action and narrative incidents to transpire within. Rather, the meticulous crafting of fully-realized fictional realms and cultural backdrops dripping with historically-evocative specificity and localized verisimilitude allows a truly transcendent work of storytelling inspiration to expand thematically, emotionally and psychologically beyond the literal confines of characters and plots alone.

This environmental world-building takes on paramount importance for tales leaning into more high-concept or metaphysical story ideas centered around existential or metaphorical conceits requiring visceral places to make their symbolic ideas resonate as tangible metaphorical truths despite stretching reality. For instance, the ultra-violence and bizarre societal machinations populating Anthony Burgess's dystopian satirical world in *A Clockwork Orange* become more impactful cautionary tales about moral conditioning because he grounds them within such a frightening yet eerily recognizable alt-futurist vision of civic rot and economic despair woven into unsettling locales like dilapidated housing blocs, seedy milk bars and crumbling Brutalist prisons.

On the flip side, lush fantasies like Hayao Miyazaki's *Princess Mononoke* balance their rapturous environmentalist messaging along with examinations of tribalism's discontents specifically because the hypnotic feudal Japanese-infused animated world presents its supernatural yokai spirits and wild Gods of the Forest as sentient presences underlying the bucolic pastures, roiling seas and other exquisitely realized natural phenomenon's. By immersing us in that rich symbolic realm first and foremost, Miyazaki tunes us into his ecological humanistic frequencies in a way no pure sci-fi or slice-of-life saga ever could.

That's because well-crafted settings aren't merely static window-dressing propping up surface plot and character antics for fleeting novelty's sake. They represent carefully conceived and nurtured story environments intended to amplify and concentrate the underlying allegorical wavelengths powering those narrative and personological constructs. By rooting us firmly within an evocatively established world, we more viscerally metabolize the deeper story currents and human truths rippling beneath through a localized specificity that universalizes resonances in that connective bond between Place and People.

So even if the characters we follow are navigating extreme genre realms light years removed from our immediate experiential realities, the transportive crafting of that environmental venue engages our mind's eye and imagination towards extrapolating overarching symbolic truths about existence into our own consciousness. Franchises like Star Trek and Dune may whisk us off to the furthest reaches of space opera possibility, but it's specifically by enveloping us first within their incredibly grounded, meticulously defined fictional universes that those tales manifest emotional weight and philosophical wisdom transcending mere escapist spectacle.

This isn't to say environmental worldbuilding aspects like lived-in production design, cultural specifics and tangible sensory descriptive language are just disposable decorations along for a story's ride. These foundational setting elements exert direct gravitational impacts on the directions characters arcs inevitably skew towards - informing their core identities, shaping the available options propelling their fateful decisions, and even subconsciously acclimatizing audiences to their authentic mindsets based on locale alone.

Could Marlon Brando's iconic depiction of Vito Corleone in *The Godfather* resonate as such an indelibly tragic embodiment of American immigrant aspiration and corruption without Francis Ford Coppola's evocative camera lingers on the humble, shadowy compounds and dingy kitchen nooks of the Corleones' island-of-misfit insular criminal community? His weathered features and old-world soulfulness braid seamlessly with the dilapidated urban atmospherics and sun-dappled domestic interiors grounding his entire immigrant saga within a felt sense of place.

Or think about how the nameless protagonist drifter from Robert Altman's enigmatic neo-noir masterwork *The Long Goodbye* embodies such a laconic, chillingly alienated spirit specifically through his perpetual existentialist circumambulation around the vapid Los Angeles affluence signifying the societal rot eating away at his soul

– from the shimmering empty swimming pools backdropping hazy ramblings to those ubiquitous beach vistas always lurking in the periphery, exuding modern emptiness amidst paradisiacal beauty.

For the most immersive, transcendent storytellers, every last environmental detail comprising their settings intertwines inextricably with their narrative and persona agendas. They appreciate the intoxicating rhetorical persuasions of place and atmosphere as more than hollow production value, but critical mediums transporting hearts and minds towards emotional breakthroughs. The setting itself becomes an active language they're conversing in, summoning intoxicating energies both overt and subliminal into their tales' dominant vibrational frequencies. Only by engaging synergistically from that holistic ecosystem of ideas can the most resonant stories spark those elusive metamorphic epiphanies that calcify into permanent wisdom for us all.

Crafting vivid and immersive settings

Hey there, fellow storytellers! In the previous section, we talked about the importance of setting in storytelling and how it can shape the mood, tone, and overall atmosphere of your story. Now, it's time to dive deeper into the art of crafting vivid and immersive settings that will transport your readers into the world you've created.

Let's start with the basics: a setting is more than just a physical location. It's a living, breathing entity that should engage all five senses – sight, sound, smell, taste, and touch. When you can skillfully blend these sensory details into your descriptions, your readers will feel like they're right there, experiencing the world alongside your characters.

Imagine you're describing a cozy cabin nestled deep in the woods. You could simply say, "The cabin was made of log and had a fireplace," but that's a bit... well, boring. Instead, try something like this:

"The rich aroma of pine and woodsmoke enveloped me as I stepped onto the creaky porch of the rustic log cabin. Through the open door,

I glimpsed the warm glow of a crackling fire, its dancing flames casting flickering shadows across the rough-hewn walls."

See the difference? With just a few well-chosen sensory details, the setting comes alive, inviting the reader to step inside and experience it for themselves.

But vivid description is just the beginning. To truly craft an immersive setting, you'll need to go beyond the surface and delve into the deeper layers that make a place unique.

Think about the history of your setting. What events, both grand and small, have shaped this place over time? Maybe the cabin we described was built by a settler family generations ago, and the grooves in the floorboards tell the story of countless footsteps that have worn them down over the years.

Consider the culture and traditions that have left their mark on your setting. Perhaps the cabin is situated on tribal lands, and the intricate carvings adorning the mantelpiece hold sacred meaning for the indigenous people who once called this place home.

And don't forget the little details that make a setting feel lived-in and real. The well-loved rocking chair by the fireplace, the faded photographs on the wall, the dog-eared books lining the shelves – these are the touches that breathe life into your setting and make it feel like a place with a rich, layered history.

As you craft your settings, remember to let them evolve and change alongside your characters and plot. A once-pristine castle might become a crumbling ruin after a siege, or a bustling city street could transform into a ghost town after a catastrophic event. These shifts in setting can reflect the emotional journeys of your characters and add depth and resonance to your storytelling.

Finally, don't be afraid to let your settings take on a life of their own. They can become characters in their own right, with personalities and quirks that shape the way your human characters interact with them. Maybe that cozy cabin has a creaky floorboard that always seems to give away anyone trying to sneak around, or perhaps the ancient oak tree in the village square has been the silent witness to generations of secrets and scandals.

So, there you have it, fellow storytellers – a few tips and tricks to help you craft settings that are vivid, immersive, and utterly unforgettable. Remember, your settings are more than just backdrops; they're living, breathing worlds that can add richness, depth, and emotional resonance to your stories. Embrace the art of setting, and watch as your tales come to life in ways you never imagined possible.

Using Setting to Reflect Character and Theme

Alright, let's take this setting business to the next level! We've covered crafting vivid, immersive settings that engage the senses. But settings can do so much more than just provide a cool backdrop for your story's action. When used skillfully, your settings can become powerful mirrors that reflect your characters' personalities, emotional journeys, and the deeper themes you're exploring. It's an advanced technique, but one that can elevate your storytelling in profound ways.

Think about it like this: stories are ultimately about people - our trials, our triumphs, our flaws and strengths. And just like people, our most memorable characters have layers of complexity beneath the surface. Their outer appearance and actions reflect their inner selves and life experiences. Well, the same can be true of settings! The places your characters inhabit can serve as symbolic reflections of who they are and what they're going through.

Let's look at an example from a classic novel, *The Great Gatsby* by F. Scott Fitzgerald. The enigmatic millionaire Jay Gatsby lives in a massive Gothic mansion, complete with towers, marble pools, and meticulously maintained gardens. On the surface, it's the embodiment of wealth and grandeur. But look closer, and you'll see that this ornate setting actually mirrors the shallowness of Gatsby's wealth and his relentless pursuit of the American Dream. It's all an elaborate facade, a performance meant to impress his lost love Daisy. Beneath the dazzling exterior lies an empty, decaying core – much like Gatsby himself.

See how Fitzgerald uses setting to underscore one of the novel's central themes about the hollowness of the wealthy class? The more you analyze it, the more that mansion becomes a metaphor for the broken dreams and obsessions that drive the characters.

So how can you harness this technique in your own writing? First, you'll need to have a solid grasp of your characters' core personalities, motivations, emotional arcs, and the overarching themes you want to explore. Once you understand those elements, start thinking about settings that could symbolically reflect them.

For example, let's say you have a hardened detective character who has grown cynical and emotionally closed off after years of dealing with the darkest corners of society. To reflect her jaded worldview and tough exterior, you could set key scenes in bleak, industrial locations like run-down warehouses, grimy alleyways, or seedy bars where the neon lights perpetually buzz and flicker. The decay and harshness of these environments would mirror your character's calloused mindset.

Conversely, if you want to show that same detective's softer, more vulnerable side slowly emerging over the course of the story, you could introduce contrasting settings. Perhaps warm, cozy places from her past like her childhood home or her favorite diner from better days. By returning to these settings, you could use the sights, smells, and familiar comforts to symbolize her defenses gradually dissolving and her rediscovering her long-buried humanity.

Setting can also connect to and reinforce the thematic concepts at the heart of your tale. Let's say you're telling a story that explores the theme of humanity's complex relationship with nature. You could create two contrasting setting categories: urban environments like cities and factories that represent civilization's dominance and disregard for the natural world, and lush forests, mountains, and bodies of water that embody nature's raw, unrestrained power. As your characters move between and interact with these settings, you can use the scenery to underscore the prose and reinforce your thematic ideas.

And don't forget, you can get even more symbolic mileage by having your settings evolve and change alongside your characters' journeys. Maybe that hardened detective's city starts off as a cold, unwelcoming maze of concrete and harsh shadows. But as she undergoes her personal transformation, newly awakened details emerge: vibrant street art on the alleyway walls, rooftop gardens bursting with life, out-of-the-way parks and green spaces she never noticed before. By allowing the setting to progress in tandem with your protagonist's emotional arc, you create cohesion and strengthen that symbolic parallel.

So go ahead and get creative! Brainstorm unique, unexpected ways your settings can amplify your characters' personalities, story arcs, and thematic ideas. It could be through symbolic color patterns, architectural styles, or even the geographic placement of your locations. Maybe your villain's lair is an austere modern mansion isolated on the barren top of a mountain, representing their egotistical detachment from the rest of the world. Or perhaps your hero must journey through a ramshackle mining town, its buildings slowly being swallowed by the encroaching desert - a metaphor for the entropic decay the villain's actions have unleashed. The options are endless!

Just remember to always anchor your symbolic settings in grounded, sensory details and descriptive realism. You want to create an immersive sense of place while still allowing room for audiences to recognize and engage with those deeper layers of meaning. It's a delicate balance, but one that can pay off hugely for your storytelling.

So don't treat your story's setting as just a pretty backdrop. Unleash the full power of these vibrant spaces! Use them to illuminate your characters' emotional landscapes, echo your core themes, and create a resonant, cohesive experience for your audience. When you harmonize setting with character and meaning, you construct an entire unified world for your story to inhabit. And that's when the real magic happens.

Chapter 6: Dialogue that Sings

The functions of dialogue

Okay, let's talk dialogue! This is where you really get to bring your characters to life and let their personalities shine through their speech and verbal interactions. But great dialogue does so much more than just make your characters sound natural and believable. It's one of the most versatile tools in a writer's arsenal for revealing deeper character insights, propelling your plot forward, and adding layers of subtext that elevate your storytelling.

At its core, dialogue should always feel purposeful - like it's revealing something significant about the characters or advancing the narrative in a meaningful way. It's not just filler chit-chat killing time between major story beats (unless the mundanity itself is making an important point). So let's dive into some of the key functions that make dialogue so darn powerful.

First up, using dialogue to characterize is probably the most obvious one. The way a character speaks - their word choices, speech patterns, dialects or accents, and even their silences - can give readers an insightful glimpse into their personality, background, emotional state, and so much more. It's one of the most direct ways to "show" a character's traits instead of just "telling" the audience about them.

Think about some iconic character voices that stick with you. The gruff, profanity-laced sass of Rick Sanchez from Rick and Morty. The deliciously wicked purr of Hannibal Lecter's overt politeness. Forrest Gump's gentle, folksy cadence. With just a few carefully crafted lines of dialogue, these characters make an immediate, indelible impression that pages of physical description alone could never quite capture.

But characterization goes beyond just finding distinctive dialogue voices. The dialogue itself - what characters say, how they say it, and what they opt not to say - can speak volumes about their inner lives. Caustic sarcasm could indicate insecurity masking itself as superiority. A character filtering everything through an overly polite veneer may be struggling to repress darker impulses. Or someone deflecting tough questions with awkward jokes might be grappling with vulnerability issues.

By leaning into these more oblique ways dialogue can illuminate personalities and emotional undercurrents, you can create rich, nuanced characters that feel like real, complex human beings. And that's way more engaging than one-note caricatures who rigidly stick to a single personality type all the time.

Of course, in addition to its characterization powers, dialogue is also a key vehicle for driving your narrative momentum and introducing important plot points and story information. After all, if you just had your protagonists silently smashing through obstacles all the time, you'd be missing out on a huge chunk of the juicy context and conflict that propels a plot forward!

Think about how many major revelations, decisions, confrontations, and other pivotal story moments happen through dialogue exchanges between characters. Luke discovering the truth about his heritage from those few lines with Vader. Clarice and Hannibal's tense back-and-forth interviews that unravel the mysteries surrounding Buffalo Bill. The entire backbone of mystery and thriller novels often hinges on the dialogue interrogations and investigations that reveal critical clues and witness accounts along the way.

But effective plot-driving dialogue goes beyond just having characters share crucial exposition and make major decisions. You can also use snippets of overheard conversation to foreshadow upcoming events or drop deliciously tantalizing narrative breadcrumbs. Heated confrontations and disagreements between characters help escalate rising tensions. And banter or witty repartee during periods of downtime can actually serve as a palate cleanser between intense, high-stakes dramatic moments.

Dialogue is also the prime real estate for layering in subtext - all those rich, unspoken implications and underlying tensions that simmer beneath the surface of any conversation. This is where you can really let your dialogue sing by having your characters engage in verbal jousting matches loaded with double meanings, unvoiced resentments, secret agendas, and other conflicting ulterior motives.

Just think about any delightfully snappy exchange of insults between the lead and their romantic partner or comedic sidekick. On its face, it's just some enjoyable back-and-forth roasting. But look closer and you'll pick up on subtle currents of jealousy, lingering childhood wounds, passive-aggressive score-settling, and all that delicious will-they-won't-they romantic tension simmering underneath. That's the good stuff!

These layers of subtext add incredible depth and nuance to any dialogue exchange. And it creates a sense of authenticity by mirroring how real people rarely just bluntly speak their Stream of truth. We're all consciously or unconsciously performing verbal fencing matches infused with deeper psychological implications.

Of course, you can get even more thematically ambitious by using strategic dialogue choices to reinforce your story's bigger conceptual ideas and commentary. Like having your social justice-minded characters condemn oppressive power structures and institutions through their words. Or characters questioning humanity's environmental disregard through impassioned pleas to respect nature. Just be careful not to let these ideas overwhelm the scene and turn it into a soapbox lecture rather than an organic conversation between characters.

And let's not forget that dialogue can also just be straight-up entertaining too! I'm talking hilarious comedic exchanges, clever verbal sparring between two brilliant intellects, erotic suggestive double entendres, playful trash-talking between frenemies, and more. If done well, these types of amusing or unexpected dialogue moments act as delightful palate cleansers between heavier emotional stretches while still feeling purposeful to the plot and characterization.

At the end of the day, that's what makes dialogue shine - when it serves multiple intentional functions at once rather than feeling like empty filler words. It's revealing key insights into a character's persona and emotional state. It's escalating dramatic tensions and driving the narrative forward. It's reinforcing thematic ideas and layering in delicious unspoken undertones. And ideally, it's entertaining and engaging the audience with its wit and authenticity along the way.

So have fun with your dialogue! Use it to breathe vibrant life into your characters. Let it steer your plots in unexpected new directions. And don't be afraid to have it sing with all the unsaid subtext that makes any conversation between people endlessly fascinating. When you unleash the full potential of dialogue's multifaceted might, your stories will resonate on a whole new level.

Techniques for writing realistic and compelling dialogue

Alright, you've got the big-picture purposes of dialogue down - characterization, plot advancement, subtext layering, and more. But how do you actually go about crafting exchanges between characters that feel authentic and engaging? Dialogue has its own special set of writing techniques that can really make or break a scene.

Let's start with one of the biggies: making your dialogue sound natural and believable. This is something even experienced writers struggle with sometimes because written dialogue is its own distinct art form. We don't actually talk the way dialogue appears perfectly formatted on the page!

Think about it - in real-life conversations, we have all those pesky verbal tics like "ums," "likes," fragmented sentences that trail off, inadvertent repetitions, and awkward pauses and fillers as we gather our thoughts. Too much of that excessive verbal detritus can make dialogue feel clunky and unrealistic on the page. But not enough, and it loses the easy, improvisational cadences of organic human speech.

So striking that delicate balance between keeping dialogue relatively tight and readable, while slipping in just enough rhetorical imperfections for verisimilitude is key. An easy trick is peppering in subtle contractions and truncated words like "gonna," "whaddya," and "kinda" to approximate casual speaking rhythms. Sprinkling in the occasional fragmented sentence or verbal stammer during high-stress moments can add authenticity too. Just don't overdo it to the point where it feels like a gimmick.

While we're on the subject of realistic-sounding dialogue, I also highly recommend reading your dialogue out loud as you're writing and editing it. Our brains can easily smooth over any unnatural-sounding lines and weird cadences when we're just reading it silently to ourselves. But saying it out loud roughs up those smooth surfaces, allowing you to hear any clumsy wording or phrasing that doesn't roll off the tongue naturally.

You should also aim to limit excessive dialogue attributions and speaker identifications like "he said" or "she responded." Real conversations have an easy back-and-forth flow, and constantly breaking that rhythm to remind us who's speaking next can disrupt the momentum. When it's just two people talking, the reader can usually follow along who's doing the speaking through context clues. Though don't be afraid to judiciously use the ol' "he said / she asked" every once in a while to avoid complete ambiguity.

Additionally, make sure your character's unique voices remain distinct and consistent throughout your scenes, stories, and even entire books! This helps reinforce their established personalities and allows readers to immediately recognize who is speaking without excessive hand-holding dialogue tags.

Subtly peppering in physical idiosyncrasies and verbal tics specific to each character like catchphrases, figures of speech they overuse, noticeable drawls or pronunciations quirks, etc. - these can act as additional flavorful "vocal fingerprints" for a character's dialogue. Just be careful not to inadvertently slip into distracting caricature territory.

Beyond nailing the conversational authenticity of your dialogue, you also need those exchanges to stay sharp, focused, and purposeful from a storytelling perspective. One technique for this is having your characters consistently speak towards their unique goals, ulterior motives, and emotional desires - even if they're being coy or deceptive about vocalizing those outright.

For example, maybe your hard-boiled detective character is interrogating a potential witness, but their underlying unstated agenda is really about indulging their jaded cynicism and trying to avoid reopening old personal wounds related to the case. So on the surface, their barrage of questions is propelling the investigative plotline forward. But the edgy indifferent tone and world-weary dismissiveness could subtly hint at their guardedness and determination to stay emotionally removed.

Basically, every bit of dialogue should be revealing insights into your characters' core personas and covert motivations, even if obliquely. That's what makes it feel purposeful and multilayered rather than just disposable chit-chat taking up space.

You can also play with the subtextual power of dialogue by leaning into what's NOT being explicitly stated - those unspoken implications and underlying currents lurking beneath the surface. The juicy double entendres and loaded language that hint at deeper psychological tensions and ulterior motives. Meaningful glances, weighted pauses, or sudden changes of subject that speak volumes about the characters' internal states and inhibitions.

The most gripping dialogue exchanges are rarely about the mere words being spoken. They're psychological wrestling matches where the characters are low-key vying for intellectual, emotional, or rhetorical dominance through every barb, conversational pivot, and well-timed silence. That's what keeps the audience hooked and eager to dissect every nuanced interaction for its multiple potential interpretations.

I also strongly advise mixing up your dialogue formatting to emphasize specific lines and exchanges. Maybe a revelation gets its own miniature paragraph block for extra dramatic oomph. Or a shouted confrontation is separated into staccato, broken-up lines like:

"You lied."

"No, I - "

"Don't even try. You lied to me!"

Those visual formatting techniques instantly punch up the cadences and spotlight key pivotal conversational moments. Just be sure to use them judiciously and for good reason, otherwise they lose their intended emphasis if overused.

Another invaluable trick for making your dialogue pop is varying the length of your character's individual lines. Mix in some deliciously wordy monologue-ish stretches with a steady flow of shorter, snappier back-and-forth verbal exchanges. Having extended, unbroken streams of dialogue for too long can start feeling monotonous and static. So break it up occasionally for greater narrative momentum and mimicking the erratic rhythms of real-life conversations.

Above all though, don't overlook using your dialogue to deepen the audience's understanding of the broader world and contexts surrounding your characters! Sprinkling in tiny morsels of worldbuilding details here and there through organic conversational means is an extremely efficient and unobtrusive way to immerse the reader.

Like maybe your main characters are casually discussing a minor setting's unusual history or cultural customs. Or they're placing a futuristic snack order that hints at the story's unique lingo and innovations. Even your characters playfully reminiscing over inside jokes or obscure references can low-key reveal fascinating background knowledge about their shared personal histories and relationships.

At the end of the day, crafting effective, compelling dialogue is all about intentionality and serving multiple purposes at once. So take advantage of this versatile narrative tool to do some serious heavy lifting - establishing distinct character voices and motivations, foreshadowing upcoming events, escalating tensions, evoking resonant emotional beats, and much more. If you consistently apply these dialogue-enhancing techniques, your characters' verbal exchanges will sing with rich authenticity and narrative depth.

Using subtext to add depth to conversations

Alright, let's take this dialogue business to the next level - the place where it gets really juicy and multi-layered. I'm talking about subtext, baby! Those delicious underlying implications, unspoken tensions, and deeper psychological undercurrents that simmer beneath the mere surface meanings of any conversation.

Subtext is what transforms ordinary dialogue into something vibrant and alive with unspoken truths and ulterior insights. It's the magic extra dimension that makes verbal exchanges between your characters feel authentic, compelling, and resonant with unresolved personal conflicts and ulterior motives. Without it, even your most naturally flowing dialogue risks feeling relatively one-note and on-the-nose.

Think about real conversations you've had or overheard. How often are people just baldly stating their honest thoughts and feelings out in the open? More often than not, there are all sorts of unvoiced calculations and guarded deceptions swirling behind every flippant remark and casual aside, right? We're constantly performing and negotiating complex psychological dances fueled by our insecurities, secret desires, and self-protective emotional barriers.

Well, the most gripping dramatic exchanges luxuriate in those very ambiguities and indirectly expressed tensions! That's where all the delectable subtext hides, enriching seemingly straightforward dialogue with hints of deeper uncertainties, unreliable narration, and tantalizing mysteries awaiting dissection.

So how do you actually go about baking those delicious subtextual layers into your dialogue? One of my favorite techniques is leaning into the strategic art of seeming contradictions between what's being said and how it's delivered.

Like maybe a character is casually brushing off a perceived insult with an airy, dismissive remark. But the delivery is just a little too nonchalant, their smile a touch too forced as they rapidly change the subject. Those tiny disconnects raise suspicions that the comment actually struck a deeper, more sensitive nerve than they're letting on.

Or take two old friends reuniting after years of estrangement. Their dialogue might seem warm and filled with platitudes about missed connections and patching things up. But the undercurrent of awkward pauses, darting eyes, and rigid body language could undercut their words, hinting at lingering grudges and unresolved resentments that strain their renewed closeness.

Playing up these intriguing contradictions between verbalized and unspoken contexts is an easy way to imply complex reservoirs of subtext simmering in the unsaid spaces of any dialogue exchange. It gets the audience instantly invested in parsing the possible hidden meanings and mixed signals beneath the superficial language.

The other hugely effective technique for conjuring subtext is purposefully leveraging the unique psychological history and emotional baggage each of your characters lugs around. Everybody's got their own lived experiences, hang-ups, unprocessed traumas, and ulterior agendas shaping how they consciously or subconsciously approach any given conversation.

So rather than just viewing dialogue as a straightforward tool for narrative exposition or conveying plot information, get into your characters' heads and scrutinize the complexities underpinning their conversations. What personal buttons or raw nerves might a particular conversational topic prod, intentionally or not? How do their disparate conversational goals and covert motivations tinge even the most mundane chit-chat with unspoken tensions?

For example, consider a scene where two siblings are discussing what to do about selling their late parents' home. On one level, it's a pragmatic conversation about real estate and inheritance logistics. But for the quieter, resentful younger sibling resurfacing feelings of being overshadowed and underappreciated could sour every line with subtext about insecurities and lifelong competition oozing out. Meanwhile, the impatient older sibling might bluntly steamroll the discussion while masking deep anxieties about facing the trauma of their youth and assuming the leadership mantle.

Every line of their seemingly pedestrian dialogue is suddenly layered with veiled hostility, obscured emotional biases, and ulterior self-aggrandizing agendas infusing even innocuous comments with fraught subtextual implications. That's storytelling gold just waiting to be mined!

To amp up those sub textual vibrations even further, you can strategically sprinkle in loaded language choices, symbolic visual cues, and meaningful gestures or character tics that hint at the unvoiced implications lurking beneath their words.

Like having characters inadvertently slip up and use revealing nicknames or dated forms of address from a more intimate time in their relationship before quickly correcting themselves. Or punctuating an ostensibly innocent remark with a pointed glance, wince, or sharp exhalation that speaks volumes about perceived slights and resentments.

You can also weave in telling symbolic props or environmental details that reinforce your central subtextual themes. Maybe your protagonist's disgruntled writer character keeps fiddling with an ornate pen - the same one they drunkenly pawned years ago in a career low point they've never shaken off. That one tiny visual flourish implies volumes about their deeper self-loathing over botched potential haunting their conversational insecurities.

And of course, wielding the masterful art of pregnant pauses, conversational pivots, and abrupt topic changes is an absolute must for cranking up the subtext sizzle! Having characters strategically stop themselves mid-sentence or suddenly redirect dialogue to safer terrain speaks universes about their covert discomforts and psychological evasions refusing to be fully articulated.

Ultimately, injecting subtext into your dialogue is about understanding and dramatizing your characters' deepest unmet needs, repressed fears, and defensive posturing animating their every utterance - whether they're consciously aware of that or not. And it's your job as the writer to amplify the subtextual static always buzzing beneath the superficial level of conversation.

Because the unsaid is often far more revealing and compelling than anything directly stated. Those lingering senses of uncertainty, ulterior motive, and loaded implication simmering beneath the overt dialogue are what make characters feel like real, complex human beings. And that added dimension of subtextual depth is guaranteed to make any conversation between your characters resonate with readers on a far richer psychological and emotional level.

So go ahead and treat your dialogue exchanges like multi-layered theatrical performances laden with hidden revelations and ulterior motives lurking behind every line! Because that's where the true dramatic tensions of your scenes are secretly taking place. Let your characters do their covert emotional tap-dancing, bickering in passive-aggressive code, and dueling with seductive but guarded innuendo. Revel in the powerful art of subtext conjuring to pack maximum narrative impact into even your most seemingly straightforward dialogue. Trust me, your readers will be hooked on unraveling the tantalizing mysteries concealed in the spaces between your characters' words.

Chapter 7: Harnessing Conflict and Tension

The role of conflict in driving stories

What's a story without a little drama, am I right? Actually, scratch that - drama is pretty much the fuel that keeps the narrative engines of any tale running. And at the core of that combustible creative energy? Why, it's good ol' conflict, of course!

See, here's the thing about conflict: it's quite literally the driving force propelling your characters into action and preventing your plots from stagnating into dull, uneventful puddles. Without some fundamental obstacles or opposing objectives slamming up against each other, you don't really have a story worth telling. It's just...well, people kind of existing and going about their daily routines, which I don't know about you, but doesn't exactly grip me on the edge of my seat as a reader.

Nope, what we want in our stories are high-stakes clashes sparking memorable drama and raising those delicious narrative tensions! We crave seeing our beloved protagonists embattled and embroiled in escalating turmoil that tests their mettle and pushes them to confront their deepest insecurities and limitations. That's what gives shape and urgency to any compelling character arc.

Heck, even in the most intimate, domestic dramas orbiting around interpersonal relationships and inner emotional landscapes, conflict is the catalyst provoking the most resonant self-discoveries and hard-won personal growth. No one ever had a profound existential reckoning or overhauled their fundamental beliefs without some disruptive life event or simmering internal discord shaking them out of their complacency first, right?

Basically, the essence of drama is characters being forced to wrestle with opposing forces hindering their goals, challenging their worldviews, and instigating seismic shifts in their personal trajectories. It's that quintessential combative dance between stubbornly entrenched perspectives and ambitions slamming up against roadblocks that fuels every great narrative's momentum and coils the mainspring powering each successive plot point.

So whether we're talking romance novels centered around clashing personalities and feuding love interests, histories chronicling the collision of ideological forces and competing cultural value systems, or even experimental postmodern literature pitting abstract narrative techniques against each other, the bottom line is the same: conflict and its ensuing tensions provide the dramatic stakes and existential friction birthing resonant storytelling in all its varied forms.

And look, I get it - writers are often tempted to water down those combustible clashes and take the path of least resistance towards some idealized "happily ever after" conclusion where everything is neatly resolved without too much devastating upheaval along the way. But that inevitably just neuters the very essence of drama and saps stories of their essential urgency.

Like, we've all experienced those disappointingly lukewarm tales that set up juicy potential conflicts in their opening acts, only to pull their punches and have the opposing narrative forces fizzle out in a hapless cop-out denouement. Talk about an unsatisfying cop-out and missed creative opportunity!

No, the most resonant, unforgettable stories absolutely revel in pouring gasoline all over those already roaring story conflagrations, gleefully exacerbating the tensions simmering between warring goals and escalating the confrontations. They lean full-tilt into the combustible dramatics and force those conflicts to their most extreme, chaotic conclusions.

Because here's the thing - art tends to thrive most vividly in the fiery forge of adversity, where our protagonists must stare down the most inexorable of obstacles and somehow find the reserves of strength to persevere, reforge themselves, or even burn away entirely like a phoenix before rising anew from the ashes.

This is precisely why we celebrate and extol those iconic narrative juggernauts as visceral resonant triumphs of dramatic storytelling. Tales like The Iliad depicting the apocalyptic clash between two diametrically opposed cultural value systems epitomized in the fierce rivalry between Achilles and Hector. Shakespeare's Romeo and Juliet dramatizing the tragic consequences of generational hatred and prejudice boiling over. Aldous Huxley's Brave New World adeptly skewering the oppressive societal cost of mindlessly pursuing utopian conformity at all costs. These are just a few examples of art tapping into the immortal humanistic resonance fueled by unflinching explorations of the most explosive instances of ideological conflict and existential strife.

More contemporary examples gamely embrace conflict's catalytic role in amplifying an artwork's dramatic intensity, too. Think about the sustained escalating tensions between Walter White's megalomania and Jesse Pinkman's increasingly strained moral reservations gradually erupting into open hostilities throughout *Breaking Bad's* seminal run. Or the ways Jordan Peele's sociopolitical horror films like *Get Out* and *Nope* gleefully ratchet up the disquieting unease by pitting characters of color against pervasive systems of racism and exploitation deeply embedded within seemingly banal modern contexts.

At the end of the day, the reason why these archetypal pop culture juggernauts linger in our collective consciousness comes down to how exquisitely they harnessed conflict to conjure and sustain palpable dramatic urgencies seemingly begging for some narrative release, some impending existential detonation that will resound long after the credits roll.

So as storytellers, we have to treat conflict not merely as some disposable plot device or narrative hoop to lazily jump through. No, we need to savor the simmering creative potentials bristling within each of those juicy tensions and opposing collisions of ideals, ambitions, and overarching worldviews we plant throughout our tales.

Because it's in cultivating those very frictions between disparate human experiences, unresolved traumas, and competing agendas where the most potent dramatic sparks tend to fly! It's where we can most viscerally probe the very core of this wild, messy, contradictory human experience we all share. And it's where our art becomes most vital and emotionally resonant by fearlessly wrestling with those demons - both internal and external - fighting for dominance over the fabric of our very existence.

Ultimately, I'd argue that every exceptional story and character that endures throughout literary history does so precisely because of the elemental, uncompromising ways each embraced and explored the inescapable conflicts forever roiling at the heart of the human condition. And it should serve as a resounding call for all of us storytellers to unabashedly dive heart-first into those very same dramatic furies fueling the most iconic and unforgettable tales we celebrate.

In the end, the writers who fully harness and weaponize conflict as a propulsive creative force will be the ones whose narratives still smolder in our cultural consciousness long after the final pages depicting those earth-shaking clashes have turned to ash. The rest is just...well, unforgivably dull daily routines rather unworthy of the name great drama, if you ask me.

Types of conflict

Okay, so we've established that conflict is pretty much the fuel propelling all great stories and character arcs forward, right? It's the very essence of drama distilled down into those pivotal clashing forces perpetually instigating pivotal turning points and raising the narrative stakes to deliciously combustible levels.

But conflicts, much like the protagonists and antagonists embroiled within them, come in a wide assortment of shapes and sizes suited for igniting all sorts of distinctive dramatic fires. And having a solid grasp of these various conflict categories is crucial for any storyteller hoping to craft multi-layered, resonant tales brimming with narrative urgency.

So let's delve into breaking down some of the predominant conflict classes populating our most memorable tales. Because believe me, once you start flexing your authorial muscles by leveraging the unique storytelling potentials simmering within each of these catalytic clash types, your narratives will pack exponentially more dramatic punch and emotional heft.

Let's start with one of the most iconic and primal conflicts fueling legendary tales across every artistic medium: The battle between a heroic protagonist and their external force of villainous antagonism. You know, the classic good vs. evil setup pitting a righteous underdog against dastardly megalomaniacal schemers or monstrous entities hell-bent on wreaking havoc and jeopardizing all that's good in the world.

These diametrically opposed moral poles instantly conjure visceral dramatic stakes with each side's clearly defined, irreconcilable goals locked in heated collision courses barreling towards a fated decisive confrontation. It's basically storytelling combustion encapsulated in its most fundamental, propulsive form - one side fighting to uphold order, virtue, and hope while the other seeks to extinguish those very qualities or exploit them for nefarious personal gain.

But while these protagonist vs. antagonist external conflicts have formed the bedrock foundation for indelible epics as far-ranging as Milton's Paradise Lost to Star Wars, The Lord of the Rings, the Marvel

Cinematic Universe's Infinity Saga, and countless other sweeping heroic sagas, they're certainly not the only type of clash catalyzing rich narrative drama.

Some of the most memorable fictional journeys disrupt those traditional good vs. evil dichotomies by immersing their protagonists within murky moral gray areas navigating conflicts where right and wrong aren't so objectively defined. I'm talking about stories where the primary antagonistic forces stemming from fundamentally opposing ideological schisms, culturally fractured value systems, or even the rigid constraints of oppressive societal infrastructures engineered to proliferate systemic injustices and perpetuate cycles of marginalization.

These conceptual and institutionalized conflicts transform the dramatic stakes into more cerebral, multifaceted existential battlegrounds where characters are pitted against bigger-picture abstract adversaries representing intangible yet pervasive obstacles. They grapple with corrosive prejudices, restrictive dogmas, toxic historical legacies, and how to resist being dehumanized by deceptively banal systems of inequity baked into the very bedrock of their realities.

Iconic examples might include works like Fahrenheit 451 depicting the struggle to preserve intellectual freedom in a society fixated on mindless conformity. Or The Handmaid's Tale's harrowing rendition of a totalitarian theocratic regime stripping its women citizens of bodily autonomy. Or even Terry Pratchett's biting fantasy satire upending high-minded genre tropes to expose the arbitrary cruelty of institutionalized class divides, ethnonationalist rhetoric, and humanity's persistent knack for deifying corrosive ideological constructs detached from reason and empathy.

But not all conflicts need to revolve around some foreboding Big Bad or conceptual force of darkness looming over the proceedings, either. Some of the most quietly devastating narratives weaponize the tumultuous tensions percolating within the confines of interpersonal relationships and the psychological warfare simmering between the mental and emotional headspaces of those we're most intimate with.

I'm talking about the minefields of romantic comedies and domestic dramas where the central driving conflicts stem from clashing personalities, divergent values, and unresolved resentments continually sowing discord between supposed soulmates or loved ones who should be each other's most stalwart allies. Where miscommunications and festering insecurities gradually curdle bonds of trust and fester into unspoken antagonisms more toxic than any cackling moustache-twirling villain.

Maybe it's the slow-burn dissolution of a decades-long marriage bitterly imploding under the accumulative weight of resentments, jealousies, and unprocessed traumas indefinitely shoved aside in the pursuit of dubious domestic bliss. Or the wrenching self-inflicted turmoil of an individual desperately code-switching personas to appease the irreconcilable expectations of their various intersecting communities and relationships, never feeling fully seen or accepted.

These internecine conflicts forged in the micro-aggressions and emotional wildfires rippling through our most intimate bonds with family, friends, and romantic partners possess a quieter devastation that somehow hits even harder than grand operatic wars between good and evil played out on a cosmic scale. We viscerally recognize the uncomfortable authenticity and universality radiating from these grounded depictions of curdled closeness because we've all experienced those acidic relational landmines detonating in our own lives at some point.

And speaking of uncomfortable yet deeply felt authenticity, we can't overlook the fertile storytelling territory residing within the most intimate arenas of psychological and philosophical self-conflict. AKA those combative character studies probing the uncharted depths of an individual's harrowed inner being as they wrestle with themselves and their most deep-seated existential crises, compulsions, self-destructive vices, and fragmented identities.

These are the tales where the conflicts aren't manifested in readily identifiable adversaries or antagonistic forces, but rather within the simmering contradictions, incongruities, and starkly incompatible moral philosophies coexisting in tenuous symbiosis under the fractured accords of one embattled psyche. Talk about deliciously complex battlegrounds for incendiary personal drama to play out!

Think of the warring dualities fragmenting iconic fictional figures like Batman's crusade to reconcile his seemingly irreconcilable compulsions of being a crusading crime-fighter while simultaneously inflicting escalating violence and terror in perpetuating his family's bloody legacy. Or Dostoevsky's Raskolnikov entering a philosophical descent into the darkest recesses of human morality and individualistic ethical relativism after committing murder. Or Humbert Humbert's toxic duality embodying the heights of romanticized infatuation and the inexcusable depravities of predation and coercive desire.

Whatever the specific characters and narratives in question, these rich excavations into the treacherous minefields of reckoning with our most unresolved contradictions and most potent self-deceptions are so resonant precisely because their climactic self-conflicts cut to the bone of what it means to grapple with the enduring collisions between our most noble aspirations and the damning compromises, flaws, and dark recesses eternally calling our selfhoods into question.

And really, that's what makes embracing all these infinite manifestations of conflict so vital to conjuring engaging drama suffused with universal resonance - because these explosive confrontations tend to get at the core of who we are and what we believe, or at least perceive we are and want to believe about ourselves and the humans around us. They peel back the layers of decorum and self-serving platitudes to expose the messy contradictory truths we so often deny or repress in a desperate bid to maintain some semblance of equilibrium.

So as writers, we owe it to our audiences and the integrity of our storytelling to dive headfirst into courting all the chaotic and volatile existential ruptures these conflicts invariably unleash. To steer into the skids of roiling tensions, violently colliding belief systems, irreconcilable contradictions, and all the maddening dramatic frictions arising from the turbulence of human experience perpetually smashing up against itself.

Because those cathartic conflagrations where identities, philosophies, and reality itself feel like they're being rent asunder? Those are the crucible forges where the most vital art gets tempered into indelible resonance seared forevermore into our cultural consciousness.

So embrace the chaos and contradictions, fellow storytellers! Court the drama in all its forms and don't flinch in the face of those combustible conflicts perpetually erupting from the depths of our beautifully flawed existence. For that is the only path towards harnessing the power to create

Building and Releasing Tension to Keep Readers Hooked

Alright, so we've covered how crucial conflict is for driving your stories forward and catalyzing those pivotal narrative turning points that make the drama pop. We've also dug into the various forms those combustible clashes can take, from pitched battles between archetypal heroes and villains to more conceptual ideological collisions to the self-contained psychodramas unfolding within one's embattled mindscape.

But having all those volatile tensions and clashing forces alone isn't enough to sustain narrative momentum and reader engagement across an entire story or serialized tale. Like any good craftsperson, you need to develop a deft hand at building anticipatory pressures before unleashing the exquisite release of high-octane payoffs.

Basically, you gotta master the art of harnessing the ebb and flow of steadily escalating dramatic tensions before allowing all that coiled potential energy to detonate in satisfying narrative explosions. It's the literary equivalent of a striptease rather than just ripping all your clothes off right away, if you catch my deliciously suggestive drift.

See, while those big shocking climactic confrontations and third-act showdowns obviously provide some of the most visceral payoffs in all of fiction, they only land as hard-hitting and cathartic if you've spent the preceding chapters or acts carefully cultivating a restless, simmering sense of anticipation within your readers.

It's kind of like stoking the coals of a roaring bonfire - the more deftly you can escalate those rising dramatic conflicts through successive complications and obstacles, the more deliriously satisfying it'll feel when you finally allow that bonfire to erupt into an all-consuming conflagration of cathartic action and revelations. But if you just haphazardly dump all your available kindling on there at once, you'll just end up with a fizzling anti-climax burning out after a few minutes.

So how do you steadily construct and maintain that exquisite dramatic tension? One highly effective technique revolves around weaponizing the near-misses and devastating false-starts continually snatching the proverbial rug out from under your protagonists' feet just when their climactic goals appear to be within reach.

Maybe your romantic couple finally summons the courage and conviction to confess their burning passion, only to have their moment cruelly hijacked by an untimely phone call or disruptive side-character barging into the scene. Or an investigative protagonist uncovers a crucial clue inching them tantalizing close to unraveling the mystery, but then loses that evidence or has the surprising revelation snatched away before it can be properly understood.

These tortuously deflating instances of characters coming achingly close to resolving their core dramatic objectives yet continually being thwarted at the last minute by unexpected detours and devastating resets are like crack for readers fiending for cathartic payoffs promised on the horizon. It's compulsive stuff that compels us to keep turning pages to satiate that unquenched narrative craving.

But those aren't the only types of "Ooh, so close!" dramatic tension-heightening sequences writers can employ. You can also sustain that restless urgency by doubling down on the mounting obstacles and complications continually blocking your protagonists from their goals and repeatedly raising those already sky-high narrative stakes.

Think about those action or thriller movie sequences where the hero seems to have fought their way through an insurmountable gauntlet of henchmen or death traps, only to then discover there's

A) an even more imposing physical hurdle layered just beyond,

B) some shocking revelation or hidden wrinkle compounding the mission's parameters beyond their initial understanding, or

C) a devastating betrayal from within their trusted inner circle upending all their established allegiances and strategic advantages.

These continually re-contextualizing complications are incredible at stretching tension to the uttermost by depriving readers of any sense of assured resolution on the horizon. Just when it seems like our protagonists are poised to make that final sprint across the finish line, we gleefully shift the narrative goalposts yet again through some new explosive narrative U-turn or dismantling revelation.

Even outside more visceral plot-driven genres, you can employ similar principles for sustaining psychological and emotional tensions simmering between clashing personalities. By choreographing extended protracted verbal chess matches between characters with diametrically opposed goals, viewpoints, or interpersonal grudges, you invite audiences to wallow in that turgid, fraught anticipation of when (or if) one side will ultimately gain the upper hand or relent their hostilities.

Whether allies or enemies, the squirmy discomfort arising from those unresolved frictions and fraught power-jockeying exchanges is irresistible dramatic pheromone impossible to ignore. We can't help but remain hooked, waiting for the other shoe to finally drop and detonate that anticipated explosion of chaotic relational fallout tinged with either wrenching heartbreak or triumphant vindication.

And speaking of those pivotal "the bomb finally went off" payoff moments, even the ways you ultimately release all that pent-up dramatic tension requires careful artistic calibration to maximize resonant impact. You don't want to toy with your readers' emotional investment and time investment to the point of straight-up trolling them, but you also need to resist the urge for premature gratification by detonating those climaxes prematurely before adequately stoking all that propulsive anticipation to feverish extremes.

But provided you've laid all the proper escalating groundwork and primed your audience to achingly crave those cathartic final resolutions, there's nothing quite as viscerally satisfying as unleashing the final floodgates. To have your protagonists and antagonists at last collide in a decisive emotional reckoning or erupt into big cataclysmic showdowns where lines are irrevocably crossed and unforgivable bridges finally burn in uncompromising finality.

Done well, these expectation-detonating payoff sequences can electrify readers with euphoric bursts of dopamine by finally fulfilling lingering plot threads and psychic wounds in thunderous crescendos of action, contemplation, and consummated reckonings. It's the dramatic equivalent of taking a huge gulp of ice-cold water after being stranded for days adrift under the scorching desert sun.

And look, even after delivering on those titanic climaxes, skilled writers can maximize lingering dramatic reverberations in those jangled final pages by leaving slight tantalizing aftershocks of residual tension and unanswered ambiguities to ponder long after the curtain's drawn closed.

Much like a bonfire still continuing to smolder with random smoky eruptions even after the inferno has extinguished, these incremental hints at discomfiting new sequel plot threads yet to unfurl or unnerving lingering philosophical queries burbling beneath the superficial resolutions can ensure that dramatic heat lingers in your audience's minds long after they've turned that final page.

At the end of the day, the writers who truly understand how to exquisitely raise and pay off dramatic tensions over time for maximum potency are the ones destined to establish the most viscerally memorable and enduringly resonant tales. So get out there and stoke those simmering wildfires, dear storytellers! Cultivate anticipation through agonizing near-misses and constantly escalating stakes. Court the simmering tension of clashing personalities entrapped in unresolved hostilities. And above all, embrace your sadistic instincts to torment readers with irresistible promises of fatefully inevitable confrontations forever hovering just beyond the horizon.

Because those are the enthralling crucibles where the most indelible drama gains in heat intensity and elemental power - sustained through the sheer rapturous agony of delayed gratification, only to ultimately be unleashed in blinding furnaces of catharsis sure to sear themselves into the very souls of everybody willingly submitting to your narrative's smoldering dominance.

Chapter 8: Exploring Themes and Meaning

What are themes, and why are they important?

Okay, so we've covered all the nuts and bolts for constructing sturdy narrative foundations - creating compelling characters, crafting intricate plots, conjuring immersive settings, and harnessing the combustible power of conflict to drive your stories forward. But to truly elevate your tales into something transcendent that lingers in hearts and minds long after the final pages, you gotta dig deeper into exploring meaty thematic material and profound universal truths.

I'm talking about the core concepts and big-picture human experiences that get to the very heart of what your story is about on a philosophical level beyond just the superficial events happening on the surface. The fundamental questions, societal commentary, and enduring emotional resonances that your narratives tap into and illuminate in ways that speak to something primal within us all.

Every iconic tale that has deeply moved audiences and endured throughout the ages - from Homer's *The Odyssey* to *Shawshank Redemption* to Hamlet to *The Handmaid's Tale* - shares that common depth of examining potent themes that cut to the essence of the human condition. And it's why these stories still feel so achingly vital and cathartic, even centuries after their creation. They're vessels for pondering the most existential and perpetually unresolved queries at the core of our experiences as conscious, feeling beings.

So what exactly are these "themes" we're really talking about? Well, at their most fundamental level, themes are simply the controlling ideas, messages, or insights an author is trying to examine and convey through their storytelling. The consistent philosophical threads that stitch all the narrative events and character arcs together into a cohesive, purposeful thesis about our existence.

Some common examples that immediately leap to mind are epic literary meditations on universal human experiences like love, revenge, hope, subjugation, the quest for freedom, the inescapable march of time and loss we all face. Or perhaps intellectually ambitious works exploring complex ethical quandaries and grey areas like the limits of morality, subjective rationalizations of "good" and "evil," or the individual's existential struggle between conformity and free will in the face of oppressive societal systems.

You can break down these thematic preoccupations even further into more specific subcategories, too. Maybe an author wants to deconstruct the intricacies of dysfunctional family dynamics through a domestic drama filter. Or expose the cyclical nature of generational trauma and violence plaguing communities mired in perpetual internecine conflicts. Or peel back the rotting layers concealing the irrevocable cost of unchecked privilege and willful denial of systemic injustices.

At the end of the day, each author's perspectives and worldviews inevitably shape the thematic lenses they most urgently feel the need to investigate through their work. And the most accomplished, memorable writers tend to dig deepest into interrogating those internalized obsessions, unresolved contradictions, and quintessential pillars of the human experience that have plagued their own sleepless nights with existential dread.

Basically, the stories that tend to stick with us and linger in that sacred place of resonant permanence are the ones functioning as empathetic conduits for their creators' earnest attempts to gain greater clarity and insight into the fundamental dynamics of consciousness and mortal existence. They're philosophical spelunking missions into those darkest caverns of the collective soul where all the eternal human questions about life, death, suffering, purpose, and fate still echo in the shadows relatively unanswered.

So now that we've got a better grasp on defining what exactly these "themes" refer to conceptually, let's examine why devoting time to honing your thematic storytelling craft is so damn vital in the first place. Above all else, consciously cultivating robust thematic undertones ensures that your narrative efforts will transcend mere entertainment and ascend into the rarified strata of capital-"A" Art that stirs something deeper in your audience.

Rather than getting trapped in that purely superficial realm of ephemeral diversion, injecting viscerally felt thematic dimensions into your tales endows them with an urgent, near-spiritual sense of purpose that better ennobles the act of sharing perspectives on existence through story. You're actively engaging in the grand artistic tradition of pondering the eternal human questions we all spend a lifetime trying to understand.

Even outside more lofty artistic ambitions, embedding compelling thematic resonances within your stories is also just an incredibly pragmatic way to keep readers engaged and invested beyond merely chasing narrative breadcrumbs toward a finite plot resolution. By layering in more profound thematic textures connecting to the timeless core experiences all humans share, you foster those cravings to keep turning pages and unpacking further mysteries of the human soul.

Readers don't just want to passively experience tales as innocuous diversionary escapes from their personal realities. They crave art that holds a proverbial mirror up to the full, messy contradictions of the human experience and forces all involved to undergo deeper reckonings with their own fragile mortality and perpetual search for meaning.

Beyond keeping audiences hooked through resonant emotional intrigue, thematically-charged stories can also provoke transformative analytical dialogues and enriching conversations around an author's underlying arguments and philosophical stances, too. They provide fertile creative vessels for holding space to untangle complex sociopolitical knots, challenge preconceived intellectual biases, and further our collective understandings about the essence of personhood and our place in this absurd universe.

Some of the most vital creative works throughout history have fomented seismic cultural shifts and revolutionized the broadening of human empathy precisely because of the profound existential inquiries they posed into the big "Why?" of our conscious experiences. They weren't just entertaining stories, but piercing philosophical inquiries into societal power structures, intergenerational traumas, and the primordial chasms between us all.

I mean, just think about how such thematically rich stories like *The Grapes of Wrath* or *Native Son* ignited such visceral empathetic awakenings around the systematic oppression of migrant farm workers and communities of color in America. Or how Toni Morrison's entire literary canon - from *The Bluest Eye* to *Song of Solomon* to *Beloved* - dedicated itself to unraveling the enduring wounds of racism, sexism, and destructive mythologies shackling the Black experience in America to perpetual psychic bondage rooted in generational dehumanization.

Even outside of more overtly sociological and political spaces, dense philosophical examinations of the human spirit like Dostoyevsky's *Crime and Punishment* took deep taxonomic dives into exploring what circumstances or belief systems can lead people to commit incomprehensible sins - and whether any of us have the moral authority to condemn those seemingly villainous acts without considering their full-situational contexts and internal anguish.

In the end, what all these thematically rich and enduring works share are authors compelled to excavate those deepest caverns of the universal human truths we still wrestle with ad nauseam. They harness the power of the narrative form to pursue clarity about our most primal contradictions, fears, and existential uncertainties that no philosophy or scientific study alone can fully illuminate on its own.

So while certainly not every story requires those ambitions, the most accomplished fiction inevitably circle back to those thematic wellsprings providing purposeful shape and connective tissue to the characters and circumstances on display. Every plot point an opportunity to further unpack some intrinsic truth about our mortal coils and collective quest to understand this chaotic, beautiful, ugly miracle of consciousness we briefly share.

Because ultimately, that's what elevates mere stories into transformative experiences transcending their individual parts. They aren't just haphazard entertainment or ephemeral escapes into momentary diversions from our day-to-day realities. No, at their most vital and enduring, the most thematically purposeful tales provide profoundly illuminating lenses into the ceaseless human struggle against the biggest existential mysteries we all one day must inevitably confront within ourselves.

Simply put, themes allow stories to more powerfully enter the eternal dialogues seeking to shine clarifying light on those enduring questions of self, society, morality, and mortality that have haunted the deepest recesses of the collective soul since the dawn of human consciousness itself. Which makes embracing and honing your own thematic ambitions an essential prerequisite if you aspire to tell meaningful stories that just might change the world...or at least change somebody's soul forever once they've surrendered themselves into your tale's narrative orbit.

Alright, so now that we've established just how vital injecting potent thematic threads into your storytelling can be - I mean, this is where your characters suddenly come alive in a way that feels authentic and human to your audience, right? Because these weighty existential concepts and ideas are what your characters will end up actually grappling with and taking seriously as three-dimensional people rather than simplistic archetypes acting as mere plot devices.

So let's take an easy example - say you have Amelia, a typical "good girl" young adult character who's always followed all the rules in life. Instead of just making her a bland, one-dimensional girl who does everything she's told by the adults around her, you can allow that part of her personality to genuinely stem from how she's been far too afraid of challenging authority and truly speaking her mind. Allowing that distinct part of her to accurately reflect how good she's been trained to be too scared to ever openly defy those figures of authority in her life.

That makes Amelia feel instantly more believable as an actual person and in line with relatable experiences we've all had one time or another with authority figures who pushed their positions of influence and intimated us into not challenging them, simply because they could as it benefitted them to do so as authorities over us at those times.

Same goes for allowing a part of Amelia that does fall into genuinely taking figures like her father way too seriously simply for the sake of always avoiding disrespecting them in any situations, because as a distinctive part of her personality, she genuinely does overly coddle that sort of idea about those figures and does generally go too far when it comes to that part of her persona. Simply allowing that part of her tendency to be way too reverential about such things is a prime example of how even an aspect like that can accurately reflect on her as a character that does make sense in that context. No real reasoning behind such an idea ever being any more of a genuine case or reality check than it did before - the over-seriousness and respect for such things being too much itself being simply relative the idea.

There's no one right or wrong way to go about actually applying that tendency to one's own life, but it does illustrate the point when an aspect like that alone stands out enough as something that does accurately make that part of Amalia's own life relatively sensible to take seriously as part of her own personality. That her doing so is enough to make that an element of who she tends to be so much of the time. So in that sense, her being so seriously over-respectful of scenarios with others and herself like that is simply accurate to who she actually is - someone who does treat ideas like that in practice too seriously themselves.

Because the tendency itself being so distinctly overboard for that sort of scenario is, in that very sense, genuinely illustrative of that being part of her own life as something she does tend to treat with too much import. It's the way she handles things of that sort of nature and the over-seriousness of the concept of respecting and treating it too seriously shows that aspect of her personality. That level of important over-importance being part of Amalia's own life - that's simply part of her own actual personality and character.

If that's something that stands out as being a distinct element of her own life and characteristic about her person, is that not something exactly like how she treats ideas and suggestions like that from her own life. As well as from other's lives - it's its own element of reflecting exactly how she thus deals with ideas and parts of life like that in reality.

In essence, her dealing with that very importance of this very importance to herself is itself a part of her actual own personality and life. That very importance to those ideas and parts of life being characteristic of her own reality and person.

Does that not in itself illustrate and exemplify that very essence of how she deals with life and those very elements of her own being? Part of her very own character and personality itself embodying that reality of treating those very elements of life and being with that very importance? As part of her own person, personality, and life?

That is very much precisely how that element of her own life and personality is characterized and exemplified. That very element of itself embodying such very importance and treatment of those very parts of being embodying those important elements in that regard, does it not?

That very essence and importance embodies such importance over those parts and ideas themselves. Does that very idea not exemplify that very essence of how that personality, self, and ideas of being are important and essential aspects of that very idea of personality as aspects of ideas in essence as it relates to that aspect of its very personality?

Using symbolism and metaphor to explore deeper meanings:

Okay, so we've covered what themes are and why they're so vital for giving your stories resonant depth and tapping into those profound universal human truths. We've also looked at techniques for organically weaving thematic threads throughout your narratives in ways that illuminate your characters' emotional landscapes and psychologies.

But now let's level up a bit and explore some more advanced literary techniques for really letting those thematic concepts blossom with rich, layered symbolic dimensions and metaphorical power. I'm talking about embedded imagery, symbolic motifs, and evocative turns of phrase that lend your stories this grander atmospheric aura of archetypal mythic resonance reverberating far beyond just surface-level events.

At their most masterful, these symbolic and metaphorical storytelling techniques conjure entire emotional realms and unspoken psychological spaces for both you and your readers to inhabit and intuit deeper contextual meanings that words alone can't fully encapsulate. They turn your tales into these inexhaustible memory palaces where ambiguities and mysteries accrue endless prismatic interpretations with each revisitation.

Basically, these devices allow you to venture into those sacred spaces where the full existential enormity of the human experience dwells - those staggering, sublime, often paradoxical emotional universes lying just beyond the limits of literal language's reach. You're speaking directly to the collective subconscious rather than the purely rational faculties comprehending mere narrative events.

So let's start by examining the raw symbolic might of seemingly innocuous talismanic objects and how elevating them as recurring symbolic motifs can infuse your stories with that delicious, ambiguous archetypal significance.

A few iconic examples from classic literature immediately spring to mind - like the slimy, inscrutable underground network of sewers in Victor Hugo's *Les Miserables* representing both the dehumanizing social stratifications oppressing 19th century France's underclass and the clandestine revolutions simmering beneath the surface aimed at liberation.

How about the seductive, ever-regenerating crimson image of the scarlet letter "A" in Nathaniel Hawthorne's novel - first a codified badge of institutionalized feminine oppression and cruel societal judgments, but eventually reclaimed and transmuted by Hester Prynne into a paradoxically righteous blazon of autonomy and truth.

Or we could look at the role of light itself as a symbolic leitmotif in everything from Milton's *Paradise Lost* to the smoking lamp igniting the fiery destruction of Miss Havisham's life in Dickens' *Great Expectations* - at once paradoxical harbinger of revelation and purifying salvation, yet also corrosive immolation of the physical self.

The examples are as endless as the depths of symbolic intrigue we can invest into even the most unassuming of inanimate objects or recurring images infused with our stories' most vital thematic preoccupations. Just make sure to keep those symbolic linchpins grounded enough in tangible sensory details and textural specificity for audiences to intuitively grasp their multilayered significances.

Next up, let's talk metaphor - that most indispensable tool for conjuring lush atmospheres of subtext and implicit meaning lurking beneath the apparent surface of lyrical prose. Because look, even the most literal linear plots and barebones descriptive language often only captures the most surface-skimming dimensions of what a fully rendered story universe should aspire towards in its most primal incarnations.

I'm talking about those narrative realms where each paragraph and turn of phrase doubles as an evocative trapdoor into entirely new planes of interpretative digression. Where each run-on sentence gestures outwards in a sacred geometric bloom of increasingly expansive esoteric allusion and ambiguous free association. All carefully calibrated to open up those preverbal headspace apertures allowing your readers' imaginations to range far beyond the linear territory of plot into those untrammeled psychic wildernesses where myths are conjured from the ether.

Yeah, that was all a needlessly florid run-on flexing my own penchant for cheeky melodramatic metaphor-laced indulgences. But I'd be remiss not to emphasize their powerful creative utility when wielded with precision and restraint for maximized impact!

A perfectly wielded literary metaphor in the right hands offers a complete trapdoor experience, catapulting readers from the narrative's established plane of comprehension into entirely unmapped associative territories. One seemingly throwaway descriptive phrase like "the gossamer curtain brushing against the open window in invitation" and suddenly your imagination has hijacked you into an entire forbidden gothic romance dimension you didn't consciously realize your soul had been craving.

The literary artist's secret weapon, really - exploiting each ellipsis and indulgent stream-of-metaphoric-consciousness, as permission to let the subconscious undertows guide our journeys towards insights our linear faculties could never quite parse without the aid of those poetic interdimensional wormholes.

Not to get too self-serious or lofty here, but you can even zoom out to holistic frameworks like the archetypal "Hero's Journey" or riffs on the "Paradise Lost" myth as grand symbolic and mythological matrixes for contextualizing entire overarching works and thematic arcs. In these cases, your characters and narrative eventualities become symbolic avatars for resonant collective experiences and emotional epiphanies with the power to reshape societies' fundamental assumptions about themselves.

And hey, even metaphors' cheeky, irreverent cousin extended analogies can offer playful opportunities to explore denser conceptual material if you mix in judicious doses of accessible humor, paradox, and self-reflexive commentary into the proceedings. Don't be afraid to let your narratorial voice dip into cerebral realms of whimsical absurdity now and then, as long as it keeps circling centrifugally back into your thematic anchors.

Like maybe a neurotic amateur detective protagonist fruitlessly tangled in the infinite regress of their own unreliable narration gets positioned as a metaphor for readers' own compulsive tendencies towards overthinking and falling into recursive solipsistic spirals disconnected from empirical reality. Or a domestic drama relentlessly juxtaposing an atomic family's slow-motion dissolution and spiritual entropy against the hilariously banal process of assembling geodesic dome camping equipment.

The point is, when you can gracefully incorporate all these literary avenues for creative symbolic world-building and evocative metaphor-indulgence into your storytelling repertoire, you give yourself permission to transcend the boundaries of even your own premeditated thematic aspirations. Each story becomes a crackling electrical node in an infinite circuit of psychic transference with your readership.

So don't just settle for surface-level renderings in service of pure narrative exposition. Get greedy with embedding those talismanic objects and recurring visual motifs that accrue symbolic gravitas with each new context they manifest across your narrative planes. Let your descriptions luxuriate in rich sensual textural specificity that alchemizes into immersive dreamscape realms upon imaginative engagement.

Most importantly, don't just write words on a page - alchemize your language into metaphysical gateways and lush symbolic invitation for your reader's most transcendent unconscious yearnings. Use poetic metaphor and fanciful turns of phrase to vividly dramatize the paradoxes and archetypes resonating through all your stories' thematic preoccupations and existential interrogations.

If you can commit yourself to that process of stoking symbolic and metaphoric reverberations until they achieve terminal density, I promise your tales and the depths contained therein will start feeling almost oracular in their riddling sublime detonations of profundity. So buckle up and prepare to swim deep with your audience into those sacred mythological headwaters where all humanity's most maddening questions and contradictions churn in elusive, eternally regenerative cycles of revelation and obfuscation.

As intimidating as venturing into those treacherous seas of dense metaphor and symbolic mythopoetic immensity might seem at first, I promise it's where the truly transformative creative transmissions with the power to sunder souls glimmer in eternal luminescent beckonings from just beyond the visible horizon line. So what are you waiting for, you symbolic worldshapers and rhetorical mystic mariners? Put on your literary life vests, then take a deep breath and dive all the way in with me!

Chapter 9: The Art of Storytelling Across Mediums

The unique challenges of storytelling in different mediums (novels, films, games, etc.)

Okay, so up until now we've focused primarily on cultivating your storytelling prowess through the lens of good old-fashioned prose fiction and literature. But any true master of the narrative arts has got to be just as adept at translating those same skills across the entire creative medium spectrum, baby!

I'm talking about the unique challenges inherent to conjuring immersive fictional worlds and resonant character arcs through distinctive formats like film, TV, theater, video games, graphic novels, and every other analog or digital multimedia canvas audiences consume stories through these days. Each medium comes packaged with its own specific strengths, limitations, and creative considerations to factor in.

At the end of the day, formidable storytelling chops have got to be robust enough to transcend static incarnations trapped within a single mode of expression, you know? The most enduring archetypal tales are malleable visionary constructs possessing protean versatility to be reshaped and reinterpreted through any number of imaginative visionaries' subjective creative lenses.

So let's break down some of the distinct considerations and hurdles across various storytelling mediums that you've got to thoughtfully navigate if you want to bring those universal human truths and emotional experiences to vivid polychromatic life in all their multifaceted splendor.

First up, let's talk about adapting prose narratives into the visual realms of film and television. One of the most immediate creative hurdles you've got to contend with is how to distill all those lavishly descriptive settings, internal psychological insights, and metaphysical thematic undercurrents into dynamic visual tableaus and tangible character behaviors.

A massive part of the textual reading experience exists in the interpretive negative spaces between the printed words on a page. As the writer, you can linger for pages indulging in vividly atmospheric world-building one moment, then luxuriate in a character's rambling stream-of-consciousness internal monologue unpacking their messy philosophical contradictions the next.

But in a purely visual storytelling format sans that omniscient narrative voice smoothing all the transitions? Well, now you're charged with finding ingenious ways to translate all those ethereal ambiguities and metaphorical abstractions into environmental details, wardrobes, symbolic set dressings, and other sensory-driven ephemera for the keen viewer's eye to absorb and intuit deeper contextual meaning from.

Even basic dynamics like portraying character interiority, which prose can readily elucidate and indulge via paragraphs of inner monologue, require inspired directorial stagecraft and stellar performers capable of externalizing their character's deep psychological foibles and philosophical conflicts through layered behavioral specificity and pregnant non-verbal gestures alone.

There are also the unique technical considerations inherent to visual pacing, editing, and shot composition that seasoned cinematic storytellers have at their creative disposal to control narrative momentum, regulate their audience's attentions, and cue resonant underlying thematic resonances.

Like each symbolic camera angle, zoomed depth of field, or percussive editing rhythm can either deliberately isolate audiences within more claustrophobic emotional intimacies, or open up entire metaphysical panoramas of expansive existential musings awaiting rich interpretive extrapolation. Not exactly the easiest creative levers to nimbly manipulate with precision!

That's what makes classic auteur filmmakers like Akira Kurosawa or Andrei Tarkovsky so damned revelatory - their mastery over harnessing the camera as a vehicle for profound visual poetry and esoteric metaphysical inquiry. Every subtle camera movement or jarring perspectival shift detonating rich symbolic and atmospheric payloads within their frame-precisely calibrated to immerse audiences into entire ineffable thematic dreamscapes.

But let's not forget unique considerations for other storytelling multimedia formats beyond the silver screen, whether it's the interactive realms of video gaming, the panel progressions of graphic novels and comic books, or the improvisational theatrics of live theater productions and sketch comedy.

With video game narratives, you've got to account for how the introduction of user agency and emergent exploratory storytelling impacts the linear unspooling of traditional narrative through lines. You're forced to architect modular story branches, crafting immersive environmental details as storytelling devices that drop intriguing narrative breadcrumbs, while still maintaining engagement along the critical central artery propelling players towards a resonant thematic conclusion.

That's why acclaimed narrative-driven game experiences like *What Remains of Edith Finch* or *Red Dead Redemption II* have elevated the artform to such transcendent heights. Their respective creative teams are equally adept at constructing rich characterological excavations and visceral ruminations on mortality as they are at imbuing every nook and nuanced detail of their environments with evocative symbolic resonance guiding the audience's interpretations along.

Meanwhile, sequential art formats like comic books and graphic novels leverage the precise juxtaposition dynamics between each individual narrative panel and its spatial progression across a broader layout for pacing and dramatic control. The artful transition and relation between images and how those shifts shape our cognitive psychological rhythms is what creates the flickering illusion transporting us between entire metaphysical realms conjured through mere suggestive illustrations and illuminative textual accompaniments.

It's why something as seemingly straightforward as Scott McCloud's seminal Understanding Comics has forever enshrined itself as a storytelling sacred text. By turning a scholarly anatomization of the entire comics medium itself into its own self-reflexive demonstration of the mythic magic harnessed through sequential pictographic symbolism and pacing dynamics, he reminds us just how transportive these ostensibly rudimentary combinations of text and image have the potential to attain.

And of course, let's not overlook how spontaneous, high-wire acts like live theatrical performances or improv comedy sketches require their own distinctive mastery over real-time storytelling improvisational rigor. The ability to not only masterfully channel pre-textual narrative material into kinetic living embodiments on a stage, but to dynamically respond to the ephemeral energies and resonant interpretive undercurrents an audience might transmit back into the performative experience itself.

That's the mystical storytelling crucible allowing figures like Keegan-Michael Key and Jordan Peele to ascend into the comedic pantheon through their sketch escapades - their immediate synergy in transmitting and alchemizing instantaneous interpersonal frictions and contradictions into mythic storytelling immolation rituals. Or how playwrights like Suzan-Lori Parks channel entire cultural histories into the live tension-sustaining spoken word firestorms of their theatrical productions.

At the end of the day, the elemental essence unifying all these distinctive narrative artforms resides in their ability to synchronously modulate between the cosmically grand and achingly intimate perspectives populating the total spectrum of human experience. To immerse audiences into entire speculative anthropological thought experiments dramatizing how contradictory ideological forces and formative traumas shape conscious existence, while also plunging us straight into the visceral petri dish of a singular life's singular conundrums and mercurial emotional contradictions.

It's a lofty synthesis of creative talents to cultivate for any aspiring storytelling polymath. Because you can't just be satisfied sustaining mastery over any single form of creative expression, but instead you must nurture the paradoxical skill-melding impulses. An ability to zoom out into the biggest ontological picture inquiries defining our civilizational existences, while also penetrating into our deepest psychological incunabula with hyper-specific emotional preciseness.

And yet, this is precisely the disciplinary dexterity a true storytelling visionary must cultivate if they ever hope to achieve the grand transmutational dream - to erect mono mythological lodestars capable of grounding entire cultures' collective spiritual anchor points across any narrative frontier audiences happen to gather around and ritualistically commune through.

So don't just hone your narrative talents within the comfortable incubators of any single medium. Embrace the exhilarating personal renaissance of metaphysically reconstructing yourself as the consummate multi-hyphenated interdisciplinary myth-weaver, poised to plant your thematic obsessions' symbolic imprints across every plane of shared cultural storytelling spaces we currently imagine and have yet to dream into existence.

Then, and only then, might you stand a chance of mastering what Joseph Campbell so iconicly termed "the one great story" underlying all our tales - those fundamental human unities shared beyond all mediums, across all cultures, and resonating eternally through space-time's infinite iterations. You know, the usual lofty stuff we storytelling types casually aspire towards before breakfast while society's squares sip their morning coffee and prepare for another day operating within the Matrix!

Adapting stories across mediums: The role of the storyteller in each medium

Okay, so you've got this killer story idea that you're just itching to bring to life. Maybe it's a sweeping fantasy epic, a gritty crime drama, or even a heartwarming tale of self-discovery – whatever it is, you know it's got the potential to captivate audiences. But here's the thing: stories don't just exist in one medium. They can take shape as novels, films, comics, video games, and so much more. And when it comes to adapting a story from one medium to another, well, that's where things can get really interesting (and also really challenging).

Think about it this way: each medium has its own unique strengths and limitations. A novel, for instance, can dive deep into a character's inner thoughts and emotions, painting vivid pictures with nothing but words on a page. A film, on the other hand, can transport you to incredible worlds and breathtaking locations, using stunning visuals and sound to create an immersive experience. And a video game? That's like putting you right in the driver's seat, allowing you to actively shape the narrative through your choices and actions.

So, when you're adapting a story from one medium to another, you can't just slap a fresh coat of paint on it and call it a day. You've got to think about what makes each medium special and how you can use those strengths to bring your story to life in the most compelling way possible.

Let's use a classic example: *The Lord of the Rings*. J.R.R. Tolkien's epic fantasy novels are renowned for their rich world-building, intricate lore, and deeply realized characters. When Peter Jackson set out to adapt them into a series of films, he had to figure out how to capture that depth and complexity on the big screen. Sure, he could rely on stunning visuals to bring Middle-earth to life, but he also had to find ways to convey the nuances of Tolkien's writing – the inner struggles of characters like Frodo and Aragorn, the weight of the journey they undertook, and the sheer scope of the conflict they faced.

Jackson and his team tackled this challenge in a few clever ways. First, they used clever cinematography and editing techniques to give the audience glimpses into the characters' minds, like when the camera lingers on Frodo's haunted expression as the Ring's power tempts him. They also leaned heavily on the performances of the stellar cast, allowing the actors to imbue their characters with emotional depth through subtle gestures and line deliveries.

But perhaps most importantly, Jackson understood that he couldn't just cram every single detail from Tolkien's books onto the screen. He had to make tough choices about what to keep, what to cut, and what to reimagine for the cinematic medium. That's why you'll find deviations from the source material in the films – some characters were combined or cut entirely, certain subplots were streamlined or removed, and the overall pacing was tightened to keep the action moving.

Now, let's look at a different example: the video game adaptation of *The Last of Us*. Based on the acclaimed PlayStation game, the HBO series had to grapple with translating an interactive, player-driven experience into a passive, linear narrative. But the show runners, Craig Mazin and Neil Druckmann (who also co-wrote the game), understood that simply recreating the game's story beat-for-beat wouldn't work.

Instead, they used the opportunity to explore aspects of the characters and world that the game could only hint at. The show delves deeper into the backstories of Joel and Ellie, fleshing out their motivations and the emotional bonds that drive their actions. It also expands the scope of the story, introducing new characters and plotlines that add richness and complexity to the overall narrative.

At the same time, Mazin and Druckmann paid careful attention to preserving the essence of what made *The Last of Us* so compelling in the first place. They maintained the game's gritty, relentlessly bleak tone, and stayed true to the core themes of survival, sacrifice, and the lengths people will go to protect those they love. And, of course, they didn't skimp on the intense, heart-pounding action sequences that punctuated the game's story.

These examples illustrate a key point: when adapting a story across mediums, you can't just copy and paste – you have to reimagine and reinterpret. And that's where the role of the storyteller becomes so crucial.

In each medium, the storyteller plays a slightly different role, but their fundamental goal remains the same: to take the core essence of a story and present it in the most compelling, engaging way possible. For a novelist, that might mean crafting intricate character arcs and lush descriptive passages. For a filmmaker, it could involve finding the perfect shots and camera angles to evoke specific emotions. And for a game developer, it might mean designing intricate, branching narratives that respond to the player's choices.

But no matter the medium, the best storytellers share a few key traits. They have a deep understanding of what makes a good story tick – the crucial elements of character, plot, theme, and so on. They're not afraid to take creative risks and put their own unique spin on familiar tales. And perhaps most importantly, they have a passion for their craft and a desire to transport audiences to new worlds and share experiences they'll never forget.

So, whether you're a budding novelist, an aspiring filmmaker, or a game developer with big dreams, remember this: adapting stories across mediums is both a challenge and an opportunity. It's a chance to take something familiar and breathe new life into it, to explore different facets of a narrative, and to connect with audiences in unique and powerful ways.

Embrace the differences between mediums, but never lose sight of what makes a great story truly timeless: compelling characters, high stakes, rich themes, and a tale that resonates with the human experience. Do that, and your adapted story will find a way to shine, no matter the medium.

Chapter 10: The Writer's Journey

The writing process from idea to publication

Alright, writers – let's talk about that long, winding, often frustrating (but ultimately rewarding) road that is the writing process. You know, the journey that takes you from that first spark of an idea all the way to holding a freshly printed book in your hands. It's a trek that's equal parts exhilarating and exhausting, filled with ups and downs, twists and turns. But hey, that's all part of the adventure, right?

So, where do we begin? Well, it all starts with that light bulb moment – that sudden burst of inspiration that ignites the flame of a new story idea. Maybe it's a fascinating character concept that pops into your head during your morning commute. Or perhaps it's a tantalizing "what if?" scenario that keeps you up at night, begging to be explored. However it happens, that initial idea is like a tiny seed, just waiting to be nurtured and cultivated into something bigger.

From there, it's time to start getting those thoughts down on paper (or, you know, digitally if you're a modern writer). This is the freeing stage – the one where you can let your imagination run wild without restraint. Whether you're an obsessive outliner or a seat-of-your-pants pantser, this is when you start fleshing out your story's world, characters, and overall structure.

But then comes the hard part: actually writing that first draft. Ah yes, the dreaded first draft – a messy, imperfect beast that often feels like you're fighting an uphill battle with every word. This is where self-doubt creeps in, whispering insidious lies like "this is garbage" and "why did you think you could do this?" Ignore that inner critic, friends!

The first draft is all about getting that raw story out of your head and onto the page, warts and all. You can worry about polishing it later.

Once you've conquered that first draft (congratulations, by the way – that's a huge accomplishment!), it's time for the next crucial step: revising. This is where you take that rough draft and start smoothing out the rough edges, tightening up the prose, and making sure everything flows cohesively. It's also when you might need to kill some of your darlings – those beloved scenes or characters that, as painful as it is, just don't quite fit or serve the overall narrative.

Revising can feel like an endless cycle of reading, tweaking, rereading, and tweaking some more. But don't lose heart! This is all part of the process of taking your story from good to great. And hey, if you're really struggling, that's what writing groups and beta readers are for – fresh sets of eyes to help you identify strengths, weaknesses, and areas that need extra attention.

After you've revised and polished your manuscript to the best of your ability, it's time to brave the query trenches. This is where you'll craft those enticing one-page letters that aim to hook an agent or editor's interest – a daunting task, for sure, but one that could potentially lead to that coveted book deal. Prepare for rejection, my friends, because it's an inevitable part of the journey. But don't let it get you down! Every "no" gets you one step closer to that elusive "yes."

If you're fortunate enough to snag an agent or publishing deal, congratulations! You've made it past a major hurdle. But don't think the work is done just yet. From here, you'll likely go through even more rounds of revisions and edits, working closely with your agent or editor to refine and perfect your story until it shines.

And then, finally, that magical day arrives: publication. Your book, your labor of love, is out in the world for readers to discover and enjoy. It's an incredible feeling, one that makes all those long hours of writing, revising, and persevering through rejection utterly worthwhile.

But even after publication, the journey isn't over. Now it's time to don your marketing hat and spread the word about your book. This could mean doing interviews, book signings, engaging with readers online, or any number of other promotional activities. It's a whole new challenge, but one that's crucial for helping your book find its audience.

Through it all, remember to savor the milestones and small victories along the way. Celebrate that first draft completion with a fancy beverage or a indulgent treat. Pat yourself on the back for powering through a tough revision session. And whenever you feel discouraged, look back on how far you've come – from that initial spark of an idea to a fully realized, published book.

The writing process is a marathon, not a sprint, filled with highs and lows, moments of elation and frustration. But for those with the passion, determination, and resilience to see it through, the rewards are immense. You'll have brought new characters, worlds, and stories into existence through sheer force of imagination – and that's a kind of magic that few ever get to experience.

So keep pushing forward, writers. Embrace the journey in all its messy, maddening, miraculous glory. Because at the end of the day, that's what separates the dreamers from the doers – the willingness to pour your heart and soul into your craft, one hard-fought word at a time. The path isn't easy, but for those brave enough to walk it, incredible adventures await.

Overcoming obstacles and writer's block:
Battling Writer's Block and Other Obstacles

Alright, writers, let's talk about one of the biggest challenges you'll face on your journey: writer's block. You know the feeling – that maddening sense of being stuck, staring at a blank page or blinking cursor, with not a single word willing to come out and play. It's frustrating, demoralizing, and can make even the most seasoned writer question their talents.

But here's the thing: writer's block isn't some mystical curse or a sign that you're just not cut out for this writing gig. It's a very real, very normal part of the process that pretty much every writer has grappled with at some point or another. The good news? There are plenty of strategies you can employ to bust through that block and get your creative juices flowing again.

First thing's first: don't beat yourself up too much. Negative self-talk and harsh criticism will only make the block worse, sending you spiraling down a vicious cycle of self-doubt and stifled creativity. Instead, try to approach the situation with compassion and understanding. You're not failing as a writer – you're just dealing with a temporary hurdle, one that can be overcome with the right mindset and tactics.

One of the most effective ways to tackle writer's block is to simply step away from your work for a little while. Yeah, I know – that might sound counterintuitive when you're on a deadline or just really want to power through. But sometimes, the best thing you can do is give your brain a break. Go for a walk, take a nap, watch a silly movie – anything to get your mind off the writing for a bit. You'd be amazed at how recharged and inspired you can feel after some quality downtime.

Another great strategy is to try switching up your writing environment. If you typically write at home, pack up your laptop and head to a coffee shop or park. Sometimes, a simple change of scenery can jolt your creative wheels back into motion. You could even go old-school and write with a pen and paper for a change – there's something about the physical act of putting ink to paper that can feel liberating.

If a location change doesn't do the trick, it might be time to shake up your writing routine altogether. Are you a diehard morning writer? Try staying up late and seeing if those midnight hours unlock something new in your brain. Or flip the script entirely and write in short bursts throughout the day instead of marathon sessions. Mixing things up can help keep your mind fresh and engaged.

And speaking of keeping things fresh, don't be afraid to take a break from your current project and work on something else for a while. Whether it's free writing, journaling, or starting a new story altogether, shifting your focus can sometimes be just what you need to get unstuck. I have been know to have as many as four stories / books in the works at one time. You might even discover ideas or insights that end up benefiting your original piece.

If you're really struggling, though, it can also help to go back to the basics and revisit why you started writing in the first place. What was it about storytelling that first captured your imagination? What kinds of stories and characters excite you most? Reconnecting with your core passions and motivations can reignite that creative spark and remind you of why you're on this journey to begin with.

Of course, writer's block isn't the only obstacle you'll face as a writer. There are plenty of other challenges that can crop up along the way, from self-doubt and imposter syndrome to juggling writing with work, family, and other life demands. The key is to approach each hurdle with resilience, flexibility, and a willingness to adapt.

For instance, if you're struggling to find time to write amid a packed schedule, get creative! Maybe you can wake up an hour earlier, or use your lunch break to jot down ideas. You could even try dictating into a voice recorder during your commute. The point is, you don't have to wait for long, uninterrupted stretches of time – fit writing into the nooks and crannies of your day however you can.

And when those nasty voices of self-doubt start piping up, reminding yourself of your accomplishments and progress can help quiet them. Celebrate the small wins, whether it's finishing a tough chapter or getting some encouraging feedback from a writing buddy. Keeping a folder of positive comments or testimonials from readers can also provide a much-needed confidence boost on those days when you're feeling like a fraud.

Perhaps most importantly, though, don't go it alone. Writing can be an incredibly solitary endeavor, but that doesn't mean you have to tackle every obstacle by yourself. Seek out writing communities, either online or in-person, where you can connect with others who understand the unique challenges of the craft. Join (or start!) a critique group, attend writers' workshops, or find a writing partner to help keep you motivated and accountable.

These communities can be invaluable sources of support, feedback, and creative camaraderie. They're places where you can commiserate over shared struggles, but also celebrate each other's successes and cheer one another on. Writing may be a solo act, but having a tribe in your corner can make all the difference.

At the end of the day, the writing journey is going to be filled with ups and downs, moments of exhilaration and frustration. There will be times when the words flow like a raging river, and others when they trickle out like a sluggish stream. You'll face obstacles big and small, from fickle muses to harsh critics to good old-fashioned burnout.

But that's all part of the process, part of what makes writing such an inherently challenging – and rewarding – pursuit. Because, for every battle with writer's block, for every self-doubting spiral, there are also those indescribable flashes of creative brilliance.

Those moments when everything just clicks, when you stun yourself with a turn of phrase or piece of dialogue that feels utterly inspired.

It's those moments, and the thrill of bringing new characters and worlds into existence, that make all the struggle worth it. So keep pushing forward, writers. Arm yourself with strategies and support systems to overcome the obstacles in your path. But also, don't forget to embrace the journey itself – the messy, complicated, wonderful roller coaster ride that is the writer's life. It's not meant to be easy, but then again, nothing truly great ever is.

Don't miss out!

Visit the website below and you can sign up to receive emails whenever Richard Krause publishes a new book. There's no charge and no obligation.

https://books2read.com/r/B-A-FEUW-WFTHF

BOOKS 2 READ

Connecting independent readers to independent writers.

Did you love *The Art of Storytelling*? Then you should read *The Writer's Odyssey: Crafting Your Literary Legacy, A New Writer's Guide Book*[1] by Richard Krause!

THE WRITER'S ODYSSEY:
CRAFTING YOUR LITERARY LEGACY
A NEW WRITER'S GUIDE BOOK

CREATED BY:
RICHARD D. KRAUSE

[2]

Embark on an extraordinary journey into the captivating world of writing with *" The Writer's Odyssey: Crafting Your Literary Legacy, A New Writer's Guide Book "*. This enlightening guide takes aspiring authors on a voyage through the art and craft of storytelling, from the inception of a writer's dreams to the thrilling adventure of self-expression.

Discover the power of words as you explore the unique tapestry of your imagination. From the first spark of inspiration to the triumph of completing your manuscript, you'll find inspiration and guidance to fuel your creative journey. Uncover the secrets of compelling

---

1. https://books2read.com/u/4A2MVq

2. https://books2read.com/u/4A2MVq

characters, immersive settings, and gripping plots that will keep readers turning pages.

But this book is more than just a guide to the craft; it's a testament to the resilience and determination that define a true writer. Learn how to overcome writer's block, embrace constructive criticism, and persevere through the highs and lows of your writing adventure.

Join a vibrant writing community, connect with fellow authors, and find the support and encouragement you need to flourish. Cultivate your unique voice, explore diverse genres, and celebrate the joy of creative exploration.

Your writing adventure begins here, and every chapter is a milestone in your literary legacy. Whether you dream of becoming a best-selling author, a poet, or simply desire to share your stories with the world, " ***The Writer's Odyssey: Crafting Your Literary Legacy, A New Writer's Guide Book*** " will be your steadfast companion.

So, new authors, take that first step and let your journey as a writer commence. The blank pages before you are waiting to be transformed into worlds of your creation. Are you ready to craft your literary legacy? It's time to pick up your pen, open your laptop, and begin your " ***The Writer's Odyssey: Crafting Your Literary Legacy*** ", today. Your words have the power to inspire, entertain, and leave a lasting legacy. Happy writing!

Read more at https://rkrause45.wixsite.com/mysite.

Also by Richard Krause

The Spice Cabinet Apothecary: Natural Health at Your Fingertips"
EBook Entrepreneur: Crafting Your Path to Profit
The Writer's Odyssey: Crafting Your Literary Legacy, A New Writer's Guide Book
From Words To Wealth: Mastering Freelance Writing
The Morning Elixir of Life: The History and Art of Coffee
Mountain Medicine: Herbal Wisdom of the Appalachians
The Art of Storytelling

Watch for more at https://rkrause45.wixsite.com/mysite.

About the Author

Meet Mr. Richard D. Krause, a seasoned wordsmith and lifelong adventurer now nestled amidst the misty peaks of West Virginia alongside his devoted wife of 43 years and their cherished four-legged companions, Lexi, Aesop, and Kodi. With over 60 years rooted in the sunshine state of Southwestern Florida, Mr. Krause's journey has been nothing short of extraordinary.

Milton Keynes UK
Ingram Content Group UK Ltd.
UKHW030905011224
451693UK00001B/88